Hospitality Cases
IN MARKETING
AND OPERATIONS

Hospitality Cases

IN MARKETING AND OPERATIONS

ANNA GRAF WILLIAMS, PH.D.

JENNIFER ADAMS ALDRICH, CONSULTANT
KAREN J. HALL, CONSULTANT

Prentice Hall
Upper Saddle River, NJ 07458

Production Editor: *Eileen O'Sullivan*
Managing Editor: *Mary Carnis*
Acquisitions Editor: *Neil Marquardt*
Director of Manufacturing and Production: *Bruce Johnson*
Production Manager: *Ed O'Dougherty*
Marketing Manager: *Frank Mortimer, Jr.*
Editorial Assistant: *Rose Mary Florio*
Printer/Binder: *RR Donnelly & Sons*
Cover Design: *Marianne Frasco*

©1997 by Prentice-Hall, Inc.
A Simon & Schuster Company
Upper Saddle River, New Jersey 07458

Printed in the United States of America
10   9   8   7   6   5   4   3   2   1

ISBN 0-13-853839-5

Prentice-Hall International (UK) Limited, *London*
Prentice-Hall of Australia Pty. Limited, *Sydney*
Prentice-Hall Canada Inc., *Toronto*
Prentice-Hall Hispanoamericana, S.A., *Mexico*
Prentice-Hall of India Private Limited, *New Delhi*
Prentice-Hall of Japan, Inc., *Tokyo*
Simon & Schuster Asia Pte. Ltd., *Singapore*
Editora Prentice-Hall do Brasil, Ltda., *Rio de Janeiro*

Dedication

To every friend and spouse not employed in the hospitality industry, who has ever endured a meal, hotel stay, or service encounter with us. Thank you for letting us be the "expert guest." We really just want the **best**.

CONTENTS

PART V: MULTI-DIMENSIONAL HOSPITALITY OPERATIONS

PREFACE

The preface is supposed to tell you how to use the book, and give you the essential pearls of wisdom needed to convince you that this book is the best thing ever to happen to you. While books are chosen by the instructors, they are used by the students. In writing these cases, I have tried to appeal to both. This book strives to make teaching, via experience (experiential education), more accessible to learners in a hospitality classroom.

This case study book addresses management issues at the operational and strategic levels. Each case also includes financial information—some cases have it imbedded in the text, while others have it developed in tables and charts. As a way of helping the reader analyze the case, an Investigation Sheet was developed to serve as a tool for organizing your thinking. This case book can be used successfully with or without the Investigation Sheet. Chapter 1—Conquering the Case Study, was written to explain why we do case studies, how we can learn from case studies, and to help people learn to organize their thinking. There is a blank set of Investigation Sheets included at the end of the book. Feel free to photocopy these for your use.

The cases are clustered by industry segments. They are written from several different perspectives; including management, owner, franchise, and the guest's point of view. It is important to be able to look at hospitality business situations from different dimensions. Each case has a central problem and a group of symptoms. Each case is based on a real operation, however, the names have been changed to protect the innocent, and the guilty, from the readers, who would probably call them up and ask them questions to find out what really happened. You should remember to look beyond the words, and think about the times and happenings of the 1990s.

Everyone wants to know the right answer. Please know that there is always more than one way to solve a problem. Case studies are 'right' when they are completely analyzed, and your professional opinion is supported by facts, industry specifics, and logical connections. You will soon be paid for your professional opinion; you must get used to forming it with varying degrees of information. Trust your instincts.

It is my hope that you will find the cases interesting and helpful.

Many great people have assisted with this project and deserve my undying gratitude. Jennifer Aldrich, who assisted in the writing and development for many of the cases; Karen Hall, my best friend since eighth grade, when we both got a 'D' in swimming class, for all your support and layout and design assistance; and finally to Robin Baliszewski who believed enough in me to work with me over the years on this project.

Anna Graf Williams, Ph.D.
email: 103327.2455@compuserve.com

Summer 1996

Hospitality Cases

IN MARKETING

AND OPERATIONS

CONQUERING THE CASE STUDY

You are probably asking "why do case studies?" Good question; we do case studies as a way of gaining experience with real-life problems and operations. While on-the-job experience in solving industry problems looks better on a résumé, we are better able to fast forward through an operation when it is written up as a case. We can see many different perspectives, and move through hours, days, weeks, and years in a matter of sentences. We are able to gain access to financial, operational, and strategic information that we may not have known enough to ask for otherwise. We use case studies to learn from other people's mistakes and sharpen our own analytical skills.

All the cases in this book are dynamic, with the opportunity for you to investigate "between the lines." There is always more than one way to solve a problem. The driving force in solving cases is to remember that we want to run a successful business. For the record, a successful business makes the best possible profit and is as effective and efficient as possible in operations and guest service. The author also considers having fun a requirement, but some people may consider this as nonessential.

The Analysis & Investigation Sheet accompanying each case provides a structure for recording information while formulating your professional recommendation. In these busy times, the Analysis & Investigation Sheet also serves as a type of bookmark, holding your place when you take a break before finishing the case. Read on to learn more about case study analysis and the Analysis & Investigation Sheet.

If you are reading this chapter, it is very likely that one of your instructors has asked you to complete a case study assignment. Our goal in this chapter is to give you a formula for analyzing cases.

We make several assumptions about case study analysis:

1. Each case will have an underlying problem related to hospitality management.

2. Your goal in reading the case is to prescribe a solution.

3. You will read the case at least twice and preferably three times, each time in a slightly different way, looking for different things.

Let's talk about these assumptions and how they work. The cases in this book are organized by industry segments, including food service, lodging, entertainment, health care, etc. Your job is to identify the problem in each case and to recommend a solution. A problem is that issue which is reducing efficiency, generating conflict, or draining resources.

Now is a good time to explain the difference between a symptom and a problem. It is human nature to treat symptoms rather than seeking out the cause (the problem). Think about the last time you had the flu. You probably took aspirin for the headache and something for the upset stomach. When you didn't get better, you went to the doctor. Your medical expert *then* prescribed medicine for the infection, which was causing the symptoms of fever and upset stomach. You had been treating the symptoms, whereas your doctor treated the problem.

Now let's take this discussion into hospitality management. High turnover is a symptom— what we really want to know is what is causing the high turnover. You may discover other symptoms such as pilferage (stealing) and poor employee attitudes. When you identify the cause of these symptoms, you have found the problem and you can make a proper recommendation. **You know you have solved the problem when all the symptoms go away.**

The cases are written from several different perspectives—manager, owner, franchisee, employee, and customer. It is anticipated that you will solve your case from the management perspective. It is also recommended that you take only as much authority or power as is absolutely necessary to solve the problem. "Don't use a bazooka gun when a sling shot will do." In other words, don't fire the person when retraining would solve the problem. Once you have identified the problem, you will write an action plan. You should write the action plan in such a way that any manager could implement it. The plan should indicate who needs to do what, when they should do it, and how each step should be implemented. Write very specific prescriptive steps.

When reading a case study for the first time, read it like a story, trying to figure out the plot. Use the floating lines along the text to make notes as you read. The second time you read the case, read it like a phone book, pulling out information as needed. This is similar to the way you use an encyclopedia or other reference guide—you don't need to read every word again. It is recommended that you use the Analysis & Investigation Sheet during the second reading. To get the best results, read the case a third time to check your analysis.

Using the Analysis & Investigation Sheet

As you work through each case, think of yourself as a consultant called in to do an investigation of a property. The first time you "look" things over you are getting the big picture (reading the case as a story). The second time you read the case, you should structure your investigation using the Analysis & Investigation Sheet. The Analysis & Investigation Sheet is organized into nine sections:

▲   Environmental Analysis

▲   Symptoms of the Problem

▲   Statement of the Central Problem

▲   Additional Information Desired

▲   Options

▲   Recommendation—Action Plan

▲   Summary of Recommendation

▲   Financial Issues

▲   Summary of Financial Data

As you read through the case, organize your thoughts under the appropriate area of the Analysis & Investigation Sheet. Your goal is to understand the property, identify the problem, and make a recommendation. Your greatest advantage is that you are not emotionally involved in the operation; you can be objective. It should be easy for you to identify "red herrings" or nonrelated information, from the relative facts of the case. You'll often find that "red herrings," taste good and are interesting, but are not important to the overall analysis of the case. A good investigator/consultant can sort these out.

(Before you read on, you may wish to pull out an Analysis & Investigation Sheet to follow the discussion. This should aid you in understanding how to utilize the sheet.)

Analysis & Investigation

Environmental Analysis—Perspective: _____
Internal Environment

#	Strengths	Weaknesses	#
	OPERATIONAL PRACTICES	OPERATIONAL PRACTICES	
	HUMAN RESOURCES	HUMAN RESOURCES	
	STRATEGIC PLANNING	STRATEGIC PLANNING	
	MARKETING	MARKETING	
	FINANCIAL	FINANCIAL	
	PHYSICAL PLANT	PHYSICAL PLANT	
	MISCELLANEOUS	MISCELLANEOUS	

©1997, Prentice-Hall, Inc.

Environmental Analysis —cont.

External Environment

#	Opportunities	Threats	#
	GUESTS	GUESTS	
	SOCIAL TRENDS	SOCIAL TRENDS	
	NATURE	NATURE	
	ECONOMY	ECONOMY	
	TECHNOLOGY	TECHNOLOGY	
	POLITICAL	POLITICAL	
	COMPETITION	COMPETITION	
	MISCELLANEOUS	MISCELLANEOUS	

Symptoms of the Problem

	Rank

Statement of the Central Problem

If properly identified, all symptoms will go away when the problem is solved.

_____

_____

_____

_____

_____

_____

_____

_____

_____

_____

_____

Additional Information Desired

Extra information you wish you had in order to fully determine the problem.

▲ _____

▲ _____

▲ _____

▲ _____

▲ _____

▲ _____

▲ _____

▲ _____

Options

Description	Consequence
1. Status Quo	
2.	
3.	
4.	
5.	
6.	

Recommendation—Action Plan

Give a chronological action plan using as much authority as is necessary to solve the problem.

1. Who?		What?
When?		How?
2. Who?		What?
When?		How?
3. Who?		What?
When?		How?
4. Who?		What?
When?		How?
5. Who?		What?
When?		How?
6. Who?		What?
When?		How?

©1997, Prentice-Hall, Inc.

Summary of Recommendation

_____

_____

_____

_____

_____

_____

_____

_____

Financial Issues

_____

_____

_____

_____

_____

_____

Summary of Financial Data

Financial Facts	Word Formulas
Time Interval	
Revenue	
Total Sales	
Cost of Sales	
Controllable Expenses	
Occupation Cost	
Profit Before Taxes	
Income Tax	
Net Income (loss)	

Environmental Analysis

The Environmental Analysis has two component parts—internal and external. It is important to identify each from whose perspective the analysis will be done so that you can determine the locus of control, also known as the focus of control. The **internal environment** is made up of those things an organization or person *can control*. The **external environment** is made up of those things the organization or person *cannot control*, such as the weather or politics. Please note that *influence* is not the same as *control*. For example, my instructor can influence me, but she does not control my actions.

Once the perspective is defined, factors can be cleanly categorized into internal and external. Both internal and external environments have positive and negative aspects. Positive internal factors are known as **strengths (S)**; negative internal factors are known as **weaknesses (W)**. Positive external factors are known as **opportunities (O)**; negative external factors are known as **threats (T)**. From this point on, use these words as defined above and not as the dictionary uses them. It is your professional judgment whether a factor is positive or negative. Identifying strengths, weaknesses, opportunities, and threats creates the process known as **SWOT Analysis**.

	Things We Can Control	*Things We Can't Control*
	Internal	**External**
Positive	Strengths	Opportunities
Negative	Weaknesses	Threats

On the Analysis & Investigation Sheet you are asked to define the perspective from which the analysis is being done. There are several general categories given for you to think about while doing the SWOT analysis.

Here is an expansive, yet not exhaustive list of elements to consider:

Internal	External
Operational Practices	**Guests**
Consistency	Perceived Value
Product	Demographics
Human Resources	**Social Trends**
Personnel Quality	Dining
Management Quality	Travel
Strategic Planning	**Nature**
Marketing	**Economy**
Product Quality	Regional
Pricing	National
Advertising	Inflation/Interest Rates
Financial	**Technology**
Revenue	**Political**
Pricing	**Competition**
Cash	Pricing
Physical Plant	New Products/Services
Front of the House	Direct
Back of the House	Indirect
Miscellaneous	**Miscellaneous**

Remember these basic rules of SWOT analysis:

1. Identify from whose perspective the analysis will be done, such as management, owner, franchisee, customer, or employee. Usually the management perspective is taken.

2. Generate an *exhaustive* list of factors to the operation. Brainstorm all factors—you should easily be able to secure 12 to15 factors in each of the four SWOT categories.

3. Be sure to *explain what about* the factor makes it a strength, weakness, opportunity, or threat. For example, if you determine that the new dining room furniture is a strength, what about it makes it a strength—its cost? its appearance? Write down the key reason next to the factor.

4. *Rank order* each factor in the order of significance. New salt and pepper shakers might be a strength, but not as significant as a million dollars in the bank.

   Once you have generated your SWOT list and explained "what about each characteristics" makes it fall into the assigned category, you need to rank order each of the four categories. You may have many items, but they are all not of the same importance. For example, you may have new china in the dining room, and you also have one million dollars in the bank—are these equally important? Most of us would agree that the million dollars in the bank is more important. You should rank order all the factors/ characteristics when determining the Statement of the Central Problem.

5. You may need to work the Summary of Financial Data at this point to add to your SWOT analysis.

Symptoms of the Problem

Another word for symptoms is signals. Itemize anything that stands out to signal the problem—use phrases or short sentences to do this. Remember the earlier discussion on the difference between a symptom and a problem. You may actually write the problem down while generating the list of symptoms. If you do, draw an arrow leading down to the Statement of Central Problem section on the Analysis & Investigation Sheet. (The rank order column on the Symptoms of the Problem Section is used when determing the central problem.)

Statement of the Central Problem

You know you have solved the problem when all the symptoms go away!
Write a one- or two- sentence problem statement identifying the
central problem. It should embrace either a strategic or tactical
problem from the operation. You may want to go back to the
Symptoms of the Problem and rank order these symptoms to assist
you in synthesizing the symptoms into a problem statement. Be careful
not to list symptoms as the problem statement. If you feel there is more
than one problem, choose the problem with the greatest impact. It is
likely that the other problems are related. Keep testing your central
problem statement by asking, "If I solve this problem will all the
symptoms go away?" When you are able to answer yes, you have a
central problem statement. Be careful not to write the solution in the
problem statement. For example, "The problem is that the Hotel XYZ
should have . . .," you are beginning to prescribe a solution. Save this
for the Recommendation section.

Additional Information Desired

As you have read the case, there may be additional information you
would like to have in order to make a better recommendation. The
purpose of this section is to itemize information you would like and/or
list questions you want answered. It is important to explain what you
would would do with this additional information. For example, you
may want to know the food cost percentage for brunch so you could
form more specifics for an income statement. By going through the
process of listing additional information desired, you sharpen your
focus. It is possible that you can answer some of the questions you are
asking and that the "answers" are actually imbedded in the case. It is
also a way to "exorcise the ghost(s)" so that you can move on to
analyze what is already obvious.

Options

Now that you know what the problem is—what are the options? An
option is a viable way of solving the problem. One option is always to
do nothing—also known as status quo. You need to describe each
option and the consequence of the option. For example, what would

happen to a hotel losing $40,000 a month? The consequence is that the operation will go bankrupt at the point when the credit lines and cash on hand run out. Give a brief description of the option and a sentence or two about the consequences. Remember to think critically and from the management perspective.

Remember, if you want to combine several options, you need to make that an option. Think of this as a set of multiple-guess test answers with "A," "B," and "C" as single answers and "D" as "A" and "B" combined. You will choose your recommendations from the list of options. You can't make a recommendation when it's not an option.

Recommendation—Action Plan

The recommendation must come from the options. Compare this to when you offer a choice of breakfast drinks to a 3-year-old. You tell him he may have milk, orange juice, or apple juice. He may not recommend (ask for) soda—that was not an option, nor may he recommend that the orange juice be poured into the milk, since that was also not an option.

Remember to use only as much power or authority as is necessary to solve the problem. Usually you will solve the problem from the management perspective. Be sure to tell **who** will take the action, **what** the action is, **when** to take the action and **how** the action is to be completed. Write key words or short sentences in the area provided. You are developing an action plan that any management person at the described level could implement. Remember you are the consultant— you are being paid for your professional opinion (consider your grade as your payment !).

Summary of Recommendation

Write a two- or three-sentence summary of the key elements of the recommendation. These are general in nature as compared to the precise actions given in the Recommendation—Action Plan section. The purpose of this summary is to allow your reader to have a type of executive summary.

Financial Issues

When analyzing a case, the easier analysis comes from having a completed balance sheet as well as an income statement for the period of time being investigated. In the *Summary of Financial Data,* the Word Formulas section suggests filling in all elements of the income statement. However, there are a multitude of other appropriate financial methods that could yield some insight into the case. At this time, based on what you see in the case, you *may* want to do some of the following:

▲ financial ratios

▲ break-even analysis

▲ trend analysis

▲ statements of cash flow

▲ any current financial analysis methods you are doing in class

This section is designed to let you set up the number crunching that does not fit neatly into an income statement.

Summary of Financial Data

The Analysis & Investigation Sheet has an entire section devoted to forecasting revenue and expenses. When investigating an operation, it is always necessary to determine the financial health of the organization. You should be able to forecast revenue and know how to read industry averages, as they will be helpful in the analysis.

The Analysis & Investigation Sheet is designed to be worked with a pencil or pen. In order to use this sheet, you need to think though the expenses and revenue information given in the case. It is important to look into the text as well as the financial statements included. This is where your professional judgment comes into play. One of the best ways to use the Summary of Financial Data section is to set up word formulas.

Word formulas do not require a calculator or spread sheet. It does not matter what software you will use to create the spreadsheet—a word formula explains the relationship of the financial elements. For instance, it is well known that a generic way for forecasting revenue in a restaurant is to take [average guest check (times) number of seats (times) number of table turns (times) number of days]. Once the revenue is known, adding up the expenses in the variety of formats they may be given in is less difficult. Each case may not have all the specific information given on an income statement, but the industry averages should assist in the extension of the numbers once you have forecaster revenue.

Your instructor may choose to expand your experience with the numbers by guiding you through financial ratios and analysis of cash flow. Remember there are many different things to be learned from each case and the financial piece is just part of the possibilities.

Sample Case Study—The Breakfast Basket

Let's try a sample case study. Questions and notes have been written in the margin, to suggest the types of notes you should be taking when reading the case study for the first time. Don't get used to having the answers included with the case! The "answers" are provided with this case study to assist you in learning how to solve case studies. Below you will find the Analysis & Investigation Sheet with information and one possible professional opinion on this case.

(Please note that we are choosing not to use a highlighter over the text. We believe that highlighters just identify awareness and are not specific enough to expedite the analysis.)

The Breakfast Basket Restaurant is located in Boca Raton, Florida, on the edge of a large suburban neighborhood. There are many other businesses around the Breakfast Basket Restaurant, but it is the only operation in a 10-mile radius that offers breakfast, three meals a day, seven days a week. The restaurant enjoys a well established clientele who faithfully come to the restaurant every weekend. These customers routinely ask for their favorite waiter or waitress, who over the years have learned what they like to eat.

Staff turnover has been very low. The head cook has been with the Breakfast Basket Restaurant for 10 years, and the combined tenure of the 15-waiter staff is 60 years. Labor costs are stable at 28%. Food cost has been maintained at 34%. This is due in part to strict controls required by the corporate organization. The property is required to send the issued logs and transfer tally sheets each week to the corporate office. The majority of breakfast menu items are mixes that require only the addition of water. The majority of dinner items are frozen, pre-portion items that require only minimal preparation—microwaving, grilling, or deep frying.

Breakfast is the highest volume meal of the day, with the Saturday and Sunday peak breakfast periods (8:00 a.m. to 2:00 p.m.), accounting for 30% of weekly sales. The average guest check is $6.75. The restaurant is open 7 a.m. to 12:00 a.m. Sunday through Thursday, and 7:00 a.m. to 2:00 a.m. Friday and Saturday. The restaurant has 124 seats, and the weekly customer count averages 2,856 patrons, with fluxes of no more than 1%.

While this Breakfast Basket Restaurant has been in operation for 18 years, it has changed hands several times, while never changing its name. The operation was originally opened as a company-owned location, but within 2 years was sold to a franchisee. The

Only one in 10 miles

Breakfast 3 meals a day/7 days a Week

regulars

Low turnover

Labor cost 28%

Food cost 34%

Logs and Tally
Sheet to Corporate

Minimal food prep

Breakfast meals highest volume

Sat/Sun = 30% of sales

124 seats

2,856 customer x $6.75 per check =

Weekly sale +/- 1%

18 years in operation

Same name/different owners

One franchise

Back and forth between corporation and franchisee

Stupid Rent/Lease agreement

$6,000/month under $80,000

Over $80,000 is 7.5% of difference

Waitstaff works from cash bags

Helps for faster customer checkout

Increased responsibility

$60.00 cash bank

franchisee generated high revenue for 18 months, before evidence of substandard practices and financial integrity were questioned by the corporation. Eight months later, the Boca Raton location was bought back by corporate once again. This happened again three more times over the next seven years. The operation is currently under corporate management.

The Boca Raton Breakfast Basket is one of five operations. The other four properties are located together on the other coast and run by corporate. Twice a year a representative from corporate visits the property.

Profitability has always been difficult to achieve within this operation. The Breakfast Basket Restaurant owns the building, but not the land on which it stands. The monthly rent for the property is $6000 per month. Once sales reach $80,000 per month, an additional 7.5% rent is due on income the property earns above $80,000. For example, last Christmas season the restaurant had $110,000 income for the month, an overate of $30,000. Using the 7.5% figure on $30,000 an additional $2,250 in rent was due.

Waitstaff manage their own cash bags during their shift. It is the shift supervisor's responsibility to cash out each waitstaff person at the end of his or her shift. This policy was enacted because of cash shortage problems during busy shifts, when many people had access to the register. The change was implemented to alleviate long lines of guest waiting to pay their checks. Each waiter/waitress is issued a numbered pouch containing a $60.00 bank. At the end of the shift, the staff member is responsible for returning the bank and cash for the amount of guest checks used during the shift. Any money over and above the guest checks is claimed by the waitstaff as tips.

Saturday, April 14th, was a typical busy day at the Breakfast Basket Restaurant. Eight waitstaff, four cooks, three bus staff, a hostess, and the restaurant manger were on duty. At 3:00 p.m., Carla Wainwright, a waitress who had been with the Breakfast Basket for 8 years, asked to be cashed out. Ken Korry, the Restaurant Manger, told her that he would be with her in half an hour, and she would have to wait. She had errands to run, so Ken agreed to cash Carla out on the honor system. He instructed her to put her bag in the file cabinet in the office and then lock the office on her way out. Carla removed the tips from her cash bag and left the bag in the file cabinet.

At 6:30 p.m., Sharon Ludwig, the PM crew chief, arrived at the restaurant. She checked in with the staff downstairs, and then went upstairs to meet with Ken about the previous shift. She found him in the office rummaging through the file cabinet, acting very distraught. He finally revealed that he was unable to find Carla's bag which contained a minimum of $650.00 according to the point of sale terminal. He had called Carla back to the store to confront her about the missing cash bag.

The money was found two days later in the back of the filing cabinet, behind a drawer. No one was sure how it fell behind the drawers. Mr. Korry felt there was no need to report the money problem to corporate.

Saturday, April 14

Carla Wainwright put cash bag in filing cabinet - Ken Korry was busy

Money bag missing - estimated $650.00 for receipts
Ken called Carla back

Money found 2 days later

No report sent to corporate

Environmental Analysis—Perspective:
Internal Environment

#	Strengths	Weaknesses	#
	OPERATIONAL PRACTICES	OPERATIONAL PRACTICES	
3	Breakfast Menu - Consistency	Food Prep - all mixes and pre-prepped	5
10	Staff responsible for own cash bank	Minimal operational procedures	4
9	Florida Brand name with multiple properties	Honor system of cash-out	9
	HUMAN RESOURCES	HUMAN RESOURCES	
2	Staff--length of service	Management turnover	7
8	Loyalty of Staff		
	STRATEGIC PLANNING	STRATEGIC PLANNING	
12	Corporate receives logs and tally sheets	Corporate Office - minimal check-in with property	6
		Changed ownership too often	3
	MARKETING	MARKETING	
		No obvious plan	2
	FINANCIAL	FINANCIAL	
1	Good check average	Lease Arrangement - don't own the land	1
11	Labor is 28%	Low check average	8
7	Weekend Business 30% of Sales		
	PHYSICAL PLANT	PHYSICAL PLANT	
6	Building in good repair		
	MISCELLANEOUS	MISCELLANEOUS	
5	3 meals a day		
4	Open 18 years		

Environment Analysis—cont.

External Environment

#	Opportunities	Threats	#
	GUESTS	GUESTS	
1	Steady customer base	Seasonal Snowbirds	4
2	Loyal/regular customers		
	SOCIAL TRENDS	SOCIAL TRENDS	
7	Very descript market in Florida	Florida population down in the summer	3
5	Florida population up in the winter	Eggs & cholesterol scare	2
	NATURE	NATURE	
	ECONOMY	ECONOMY	
6	Boca Raton - solid economic base	Inflation - costs go up	5
	TECHNOLOGY	TECHNOLOGY	
8	Cost of technology going down		
	POLITICAL	POLITICAL	
9	Tax laws		
	COMPETITION	COMPETITION	
3	Only restaurant in the area serving breakfast	Growth in the area - makes it prime for	1
4	Few restaurants in the area	new restaurants	
		Franchise operations increasing in area	6
	MISCELLANEOUS	MISCELLANEOUS	

©1997, Prentice-Hall, Inc.

Symptoms of the Problem

	Rank
Profitability is difficult to achieve	3
Poor cash out systems	4
Missing money	5
Leasing arrangements	1
Ownership keeps changing	6
Management turnover	2

Statement of the Central Problem

If properly identified, all symptoms will go away when the problem is solved.

The Breakfast Basket Restaurant lacks standard procedures and operational controls.

Additional Information Desired

Extra information you wish you had in order to fully determine the problem.

▲ Who designed the operational procedures - parent company or franchisee?

▲ Who signed the stupid lease arrangement - corporation or franchisee?

▲ How successful are the other Breakfast Basket franchises?

▲ Like to know the direct operating figure (income statement).

▲

▲

▲

▲

Options

Description	Consequence
1. **Status Quo** - Keep operations the same	No improvement—spotty minimal profit
2. Redo the cash out procedures	Money handling procedures would reduce in efficiency
3. Standardize all operational procedures at the store level	Improved cash handing and kitchen operations
4. Standardize all operational procedures from the corporate level	Reorganization of the Breakfast Basket— improved operations and profit
5. Fire the Manager	Legal implications and the chance to start over

©1997, Prentice-Hall, Inc.

Recommendation—Action Plan

Give a chronological action plan, using as much authority as is necessary to solve the problem.

1.	Who? - *Corporate District Manager* When? *Immediately*	What? *Audit the procedures of the Boca Ratan Breakfast Basket* How? *Bring in a team with expertise in kitchen operations, cash control systems, overall restaurant operations, and strategic planning.*
2.	Who? *The Corporate Investigation Team* When? *During their visit*	What? *Interview all staff* How? *Explain why the audit of the property Invite participation from everyone*
3.	Who? *Corporate District Manager* When? *ASAP*	What? *Supervises and generates the report on the Breakfast Basket audit* How? *Summarize interview and strive to write operating standards and cleanly communicate policies.*
4.	Who? *Franchise* When? *Immediately*	What? *Should review the franchise agreement for services provided* How? *Check for the services and requirements of the agreement to see who will pay for the audit and what the obligations are for compliance.*
5.	Who? *Corporate Office/Parent Company & Franchisee* When? *ASAP - 2 weeks*	What? *Reconcile the report with the franchisee* How? *Reconcile the agreement for the new operational practices -- begin to apply as soon as possible.*
6.	Who? When?	What? How?

©1997, Prentice-Hall, Inc.

■ 26 ■

Summary of Recommendation

Standardize all operational procedures from the corporate level. Work to develop operational

procedures which will standardize the cashout, kitchen, and front of the house services,

without negatively impacting the guests. This practice may include investigating the current

lease arrangement.

Financial Issues

Do more analysis on the lease agreement - Last Christmas season the restaurant had an

$110,000 income for the month, an overate of $30,000. Using the 7.5% figure on $30,000,

additional $2,250 in rent was due.

Summary of Financial Data

Financial Facts	Word Formulas
Time Interval—	Current
Revenue	
	Number of Guests X Ave. Guest Check X number of weeks
Food	2856 x $6.75 x 52 =
	$1,002,456.00
Total Sales	$1,002,456.00
Cost of Sales	Total Sales x 34%
	$1,002,456.00 x .34 = 340,835.04
Gross Profit	Total Sales - Cost of Sales
	$1,002,456.00 - 340,835.04 = $661,620.96
Controllable Expenses	
Labor Expenses	Total Sales x Labor Cost%
	$1,002,456.00 x .28 = $280,687.68
Occupation Cost	
Rent	Monthly Rent x 12 months
	$6,000 x 12 = $72,000
Additional Rent	Revenue over $80,000 x .075 Calculated on a per month basis
Profit Before Taxes	
Income Tax	
Net Income (loss)	

> **More information can be filled in by working from the industry averages.**
>
> **Break Even Analysis could be appropriate on the Rent Formulas.**

©1997, Prentice-Hall, Inc.

KENT'S FAMILY RESTAURANT

John Kent opened Kent's Family Restaurant in 1973. Mr. Kent grew up in a closely knit farm family which placed a heavy emphasis on hard work and loyalty. After finishing high school, he continued to work on the family farm where he had a knack for fixing machinery and for supervising employees.

After several years, he met and married Judy Drysdale, who had graduated from Kansas State with a Home Economics degree. Following graduation she had co-managed a small sandwich shop in the business distract of Wichita. Mrs. Kent was in large part the inspiration for Mr. Kent's decision to stop working on the family farm and to establish his own business.

The Kents were able to finance the restaurant primarily with the money they had saved by living and working on the family farm. However, they still needed $40,000, which Mrs. Kent borrowed from her family. Mr. Kent placed a priority on paying back the loan, even though Mrs. Kent's family assured him that it was not necessary. They were able to pay back the $40,000 loan with interest within four years.

The Kent's Family Restaurant opened in the Fall-of 1973, outside of Wichita, Kansas, on Route 57. Route 57 is a heavily traveled road just off the interstate. The majority of traffic on the road is en route between the residential community located 15 miles south of the restaurant and the on-ramp to the interstate located 2 miles east of the restaurant.

There are very few other business located in the vicinity of Kent's Restaurant although the area has been commercially zoned. Directly across the road is a 4-acre undeveloped parcel of land which has been on the market for the past five years. The two closest businesses to the restaurant are Pfisters International, a privately owned farm implement and truck part dealership, and Walter Communications, a telecommunications company that specializes in cellular phones.

Over the years the business has improved and grown to the point where for the past several years Friday and Saturday nights have had a forty-five-minute to one-hour wait. The Kents have operated the business as a "family affair." Mr. Kent supervises the front of the house operations, while Mrs. Kent has been instrumental to the kitchen operations. The Kents expected all of their children to work part time in the business while growing up. By the end of their high school years, each of their four children developed some expertise in the family business.

The interior of the restaurant is brightly lit with high ceilings and is contemporary in its layout and design. Mr. and Mrs. Kent have adhered to a once every ten year renovation schedule and have budgeted accordingly. The building the restaurant is housed in was a new construction on a lovely rural piece of land in the early 1970s and close to their home. Both of the Kents were very pleased with the layout and design and construction of their restaurant. The facility has a generous curb cut and ample parking.

The restaurant menu concept was based upon family dining. Mr. Kent enjoyed taking his family out and eating together; he and his wife wanted to create the same type of atmosphere in their business. Mr. Kent constantly reminded staff that guests were to be treated as if they were "guests in their own homes," guests that had the potential of leaving them well provided for in their wills. This 120-seat restaurant is a mixture of both booths and tables with only a secondary liquor license to save money. Beer and wines are the only forms of alcohol served in the restaurant. Careful training and rigid policies ensure that staff are oriented to guest consumption patterns.

Kent's Family Restaurant is noted for its generous cut of Prime Rib and homemade biscuits. Other strong sellers on the menu are a rich Cream of Mushroom Soup and year round homemade ice cream and cookies. The menu is based upon a single pricing strategy which has evolved from a table d'hôte to a modified a la carte structure. The take- out business is beginning to expand.

The Kents began this strategy in the 1970s by offering a salad, entree with starch and vegetable, dessert, and beverage for $8.95 a person. After the first renovation of the restaurant in 1983, the first change to pricing structure was made. Through the 1980s, the price increased to $9.99 and included a choice of soup or salad, an entree with starch and vegetable, and a choice of beverage. Following the 1993 renovation, the dinner package evolved to a choice of soup or salad, and entree with starch and vegetable at the price of $10.95. The Kent's decision to remove beverages from the "dinner package" was driven by the margin to be gained in beverage sales.

Although Kent's Family Restaurant has maintained acceptable levels of profitability since the most recent renovation, there have been a number of challenges on both the business and personal fronts. The price increase and change to the "dinner package" were not well received by some of the established clientele. In addition, Brickers' Home Style chain specializing in eat-in/take-out "comfort" food and rotisserie chicken has opened about 20 miles south of the Kent restaurant. The chain is known for its valuable coupons, which are distributed in the local Sunday paper.

In terms of the management of the restaurant, Mr. Kent has remained the key management strength for the front of the house operations. However due to the family crisis 18 months ago, additional management staff was hired to assist in overseeing front and back of the house operations. An assistant restaurant manager was hired to run the dining room in Mr. Kent's absence, and an Executive Chef was hired to take over kitchen operations.

Eighteen months ago, while taking inventory of the homemade ice cream in the walk-in freezer, Mrs. Kent wrenched her back catching a falling 40-lb. box. While the initial diagnosis indicated a short-term injury, to date Mrs. Kent has been unable to return to work. The family has recently been informed that the injury will be permanent.

Faced with a declining customer base, Mr. Kent sought the advice of the Executive Chef who had worked several years in industry for a hotel as the executive chef. The Executive Chef, Ricardo Spatzel, chose to leave the hotel because he wanted to have autonomy in all decision making. When Chef Spatzle joined the Kent's Family Restaurant, he knew that he would share in the decision making, but would have autonomy in daily operations. After six months at the restaurant, the chef prepared a proposal recommending that restaurant be expanded to include a separate function room. This would allow Kent's to attract function business on a regular basis: the focus would be for wedding, anniversary, graduations, and club functions. In the past, small functions had been held in the main dining room, but there was little repeat business because of the lack of privacy.

Construction on the addition to the restaurant began 3 months ago and is near completion. Mr. Kent is paying cash for the construction. It is anticipated that the construction will cost approximately $150,000. He believes that this will turn around some of the downside they have been experiencing recently. The new addition provides for a 100-seat banquet room with dance floor, a large storage area, office space, and an independent banquet kitchen, connected by a single corridor to the main kitchen. The new function room has a separate curb-cut and guest entrance. There are no connecting doors between the restaurant dining room and the new function room in the front of the house. As a result, staff must enter the new addition through the kitchen.

Even though construction is nearly completed, Mrs. Kent is now becoming concerned over feasibility of the construction and the depletion of the business cash reserves. Chef Spatzle has tried to reassure Mr. Kent that Mrs. Kent's concerns are unfounded and that ample business will be generated from both social (from the residential community) and business (Walter Communications) functions. As a result of the competing interests of Mrs. Kent and Chef Spatzle, the working relationships within the restaurant operations have become stressed.

Mrs. Kent has historically handled all advertising and promotion for the Kent Family Restaurant. She and Mr. Kent have always made joint decisions regarding advertising, financial management, and the overall direction of the business. Advertising for the new room needs to be more than it has been in the past ($20,000/year). Public relations has always come from the good will created through community events.

There are a few unbending mutual decision rules in place. Rule number one is that they will never borrow money again. Rule number two is that service of the guests must never be compromised. And rule number three dictates that the menu must be centered around beef.

Mrs. Kent has had an evolving plan where a small add runs in the Sunday paper every week. Her purpose in doing this is to keep up awareness of their business with the public. In addition, they have two billboards which give directions from the interstate to the restaurant. Mrs. Kent has always remained committed to charity work. The Special Olympics and local food bank benefit from two sponsorships a year providing food and workers from the restaurant. On several occasions the restaurant has been reviewed by the local food editor who thinks they have great food with a high perceived value. The editor reports that friends and families meet at Kent's Family Restaurant often. The word of mouth advertising is the lifeblood of the business according to Mr. Kent, who prides himself in greeting every table during the evening sittings.

Prior to the accident, Mr. and Mrs. Kent discussed much of the planning for the operations at home. Now, Mr. Kent makes the decisions at the restaurant to avoid creating undue stress for his wife.

The business is stable with minimal seasonal flex. The new banquet facilities are as of yet untested. Intuition, which has historical been good, has driven the decision to add on and expand.

Kent Family Restaurant

Income Statement 1992 - 1994

	1994		1993		1992
Food Sales	$1,211,760		$1,101,600		$1,000,080
Beverage Sales	$73,440		$70,040		$74,000
Total Sales	**$1,285,200**		**$1,171,640**		**$1,074,080**
Payroll	$270,080		$250,890		$220,980
Employee Benefits	$51,760		$49,670		$47,050
Advertising & Promotion	$20,000		$20,000		$20,000
Repairs & Maintenance	$18,000		$17,000		$19,000
Direct Operating	$51,000		$50,000		$48,000
Administration & General	$90,086		$89,700		$87,050
Utilities	$34,000		$31,000		$29,000
Total	**$534,926**		**$508,260**		**$471,080**
Food Cost	$389,000		$345,000		$340,000
Beverage Cost	$10,000		$12,000		$12,450
Total Food & Bev Cost	**$399,000**		**$357,000**		**$352,450**
Liquor License	$2,025		$2,000		$2,000
Insurance	$18,000		$16,000		$16,000
Rentals	$600		$450		$578
Property Tax	$7,000		$5,900		$5,900
Other Income (Expense)	$0		$0		$0
Total	**$20,025**		**$18,000**		**$18,000**
Profit Before Taxes	$331,249		288,380		232,550
Income Tax	$109,312		$95,165		$76,742
Net Income	$221,937		$ 193,215		$155,808

3

BRENTLY-ZITCH CORPORATION

Background

Las Vegas, NV

This is a day in the life of Tayla Zitch, a very successful hospitality business woman. This case includes the decisions she faces, as well as the typical communications of a day. This case is written from Tayla Zitch's point of view.

Name: Tayla Zitch. Owner/President

Age: 43 years old

Born & raised: Kissimee, FL

First business: *The Wooden Nickel,* founded 9 years ago with $200,000 inheritance from my grandmother, Aleeta Brently.

Last Year: Gross Profit of 28 million dollars.

Corp. Headquarters: Las Vegas, NV

Focus: "Eatertainment"

▲ Eating and entertainment are the future.

▲ "Going out to indulge"

▲ People will "be good" at home, but they want to "be bad" when they go out. Give them options that they would normally deny themselves—extra thick steaks, mashed potatoes with extra gravy, pecan rolls, double decker chocolate cheese cake.

Employees: 290-ish employees; of those 71 are salaried positions.

Business Anchors:

The Wooden Nickel (210 seats)—known for great meals at great prices, salad bar, fantastic desserts.

Average Lunch Check : $7.00.

Average Dinner Check: $11.00

4 locations in the Las Vegas area.

The Turquoise Grille (135 seats)—noted for elegance, traditional fare, ample portions.

Average Lunch Check: $27.00

Average Dinner Check: $65.00

3 locations in the Las Vegas

Secrets to Success:

1. Find and keep the right life partner.

2. Family is central to everything. (I have two sons, Theobald and Alexander).

3. Stay in touch.

    ▲Read everything you can get your hands on (reads 3 papers a day, 100 publications a month).

    ▲Cybersurfing (2 hours a day on the Internet, electronic journals).

4. Maintain balance in your life.

5. Love what you do.

6. Surround yourself with great people.

7. Listen to your employees and guests.

Food and Beverage Operations

Community Service Efforts: The Serve Your Choice Campaign—1% of each guest check is donated to a non-profit agency that the guest chooses from a list on the back of the guest check.

The Future:

Expansion plans for Phoenix area
Franchising *The Turquoise Grill*
Carry out expansion for *The Wooden Nickel*

A Day in the Life of Tayla Zitch

"The morning begins at 8 a.m. as I drink my coffee and collect my thoughts." I need to expand my two established businesses -- the "Nickel" and the "Grille." Both concepts compliment one another through a central commissary and bulk contracts. Most people in the area, when they think of eating beef, think of us. My lawyer, Paul Ward, is working on the franchise agreement for the Grille. There has been good growth in the mid-90s, with both operations averaging at 7% net profit. The industry averages suggest that a minimum 6% profit margin is possible in most beef operations. I believe other people would also like to share in this concept, especially with the increased interest in beef. The Grille contributes a significant amount of profit to my bottom line. The key to the success of the Turquoise Grille is knowing the guests. We have found through market research that only 40% of our guests are here because they are visiting the Vegas strip. The majority of guests are well-entrenched community people. Interestingly enough, only 20% of our business is because of celebrations like anniversary or birthdays. There is a well-established business community with an interest in fine food. This mixture of market research tells me that people dine with us because of the food and the perceived value. Over 55% of our guests are repeat. The Nickel, while in a great location, has fallen victim to robberies due to its success."

"We are glad to be located in the Las Vegas area because of the economic growth in the area. My competitors are successful, and so are the "Nickel" and the "Grille." I usually position my restaurants where there are a variety of types of restaurants with varied concepts. Some of my biggest competitors are the great restaurant operations within the hotels on the strip. You have to really work to stand out in the local community. Brand name recognition works well for my restaurants. Location is important, but advertising and guest service are more important. Las Vegas is forecasted to be one of the greatest places to dine in the country by the year 2000. The area has the promise of attracting great new concepts and many franchises."

"Back to the mail . . . rather the fax."

Dear Tayla,

Just a quick note to let you know I have two interesting restaurant concepts which have come across my desk in the past two days, and may just be what you have been looking for to expand. Both of the concepts are non-traditional in their approach, and as you are fond of saying "border on the lunatic fringe." Yet, forecasts for both operations are promising. In addition to the profiles, I have included demographic profiles of potential customers for each project. A unique aspect of both of these proposals, is the opportunity to incorporate a retail shop into the restaurant design. This would afford the opportunity to see proprietary merchandise —T-shirts, hats, books, mugs, etc., and related products associated with the restaurant.

I will be back in town on Friday morning. I will give you a call then, and we can arrange a meeting time to discuss these ideas further. Sincerely, *Paul Ward*

"I can always count on Paul sending me something non-traditional and usually entertaining. Lets see what we have here—*The Internet Cafe* and *The Brew Buck Pub*. Well, from the names alone, it is easy to see that we are dealing with very different concepts."

The Brew Buck Pub

"The Brew Buck Pub proposal describes a fun-filled atmosphere targeted at the late 20s through the late 40s crowd. The decor is described as country–western, with unfinished wall and ceiling beams, hardwood floors, natural fibers for window treatments, and seat cushions. Seating in the main dining room is comprised of large booths, and tables. This will allow maximum flexibility in seating arrangements, as the Brew Pub is anticipated to appeal to groups of friends/ "double dates" rather than to single diners or couples. Average guest check is projected to be $9.50. Full plate glass windows on the right-hand side of the dining room display the brewing process. Three large stainless steel vats are visible. Shelving, seen through the glass, display the major ingredients in each of the beers in process, as well as a decorative bottle and stein display".

"The brew pub has projected seating for 146 seats in the dining room, with an adjacent pub room seating 40 patrons. The pub room serves as an overflow area during peak times, and as a gathering place when the main dining room is closed. The menu centers on familiar foods with interesting twists—for example Grilled Chicken Sandwiches served with tomato-onion chutney; Thanksgiving Delights with smoked turkey and cranberries; burgers with gourmet toppings; and bratwurst steamed in beer served with Apple Sauerkraut. In addition to the entree selection, the menu proposal offers several appetizers, with the option of full or half orders. I like the suggested offerings because it balances the 'fried food muchycrunchies' with more healthful offerings. Offering guests the option of full or half orders is intended to encourage them to order 2 or 3 half orders of a variety of appetizers rather than one full order, thus increasing the guest check.

"The atmosphere of the pub is meant to be up-beat and playful. Staffing is the key to achieving this. To foster a 'trademark' image of the brew pub, they describe the staff is a team of young men and women exemplifying the 'All-American Image' of health and fitness. Young men, or the Brew Bucks, as the proposal refers to them, form the core of the waitstaff team. Uniforms for the men will be khaki shorts with sleeveless oxford button down shirts. The back of the shirt will be silk-screened with *The Brew Buck Pub* logo, while printed on the front pocket will be the phrase—*"Let me FROST your MUG."* Young women will be employed primarily as Bartenders, Barbacks, bus staff, kitchen staff or as hostesses. Their uniforms will be similar to those of the men, but rather than a full length oxford shirt, theirs will be tailored to be tied at the waist.

"The proposal projects that the "Brew Bucks" will be exceedingly popular and will serve as a major drawing point especially for young women. Merchandising opportunities are tremendous for this operation. Not only will there be opportunities for proprietary merchandise, but also for beer-making kits, bottles, and recipe books."

The Internet Cafe

"The Internet Cafe takes a more 'new age' approach. The Cafe will offer 24-hour-a-day service and is primarily targeted at the single-person market. This contrasts with the Brew pub's niche which is directly targeted at parties of three or more. The atmosphere will be a blend of futuristic "Star Trek" with an old library. Areas of the dining room designed for quiet reading are separated from the rest of the dining room by large bookcases that face inward toward the reading area. The back side of the bookcases will be painted with 'techno-pictures' appropriate to the theme of the Cafe. The seating capacity of the Internet Cafe will be 165 guests—45 seats in the 'library' and the remainder in the 'Techno' dining room. The average guest check is projected to be $8.37. Ergonomically correct computer stations, providing access to the Internet, CompuServe, and America On Line, will be equipped with specially designed keyboard shields to protect the equipment from food and/or liquid consumed at the stations.

"The Internet Cafe is positioned to attract the computer literate guest, however supports workshops, lessons and reference books offered for sale to initiate the non-user to the wonders of 'Cyberspace.' There will be 10 stations with "House Accounts," and another 10 stations available for users, with their own accounts to log on and use their own resources. The House Accounts will focus on access to the Internet, but other computer services will be offered. The stations will accommodate one person working at the keyboard, with up to three more people watching. Half of the stations will be equiped with large screen monitors, while the other half will remain standard size for privacy. Printers will be available at each station, and the first 10 pages can be printed free of charge. The first 30 minutes on line will be free to each party. After 30 minutes, there will be a charge of $5.00 per 1/2 hour, or a minimum food order of $7.00 per half hour. Patrons using only the library facilities must make a minimum food purchase of $7.00.

"The menu at the Internet Cafe will center around healthful, all natural foods. Priority will be placed on using only organically raised produce and meats.

Whole grain and stuffed breads baked on site, soups, stews, and hearty sandwiches will form the core of the menu. Appetizers and a broad range of pastries will be offered. Alcohol will not be served at the Internet cafe. Beverages offered will consist of gourmet coffees and teas, espresso, cappuccino, etc., fresh squeezed fruit juices, and bottled waters.

"Because of the unique nature of the Cafe, it is critical that staff have excellent hospitality skills and be computer literate, with the ability to 'Surf the Net.' Part of the staff's responsibility will be in 'up-selling' the Internet to guests that may be unfamiliar with 'cyber-space'. The proposal suggests that part of the screening process for staff include a computer proficiency test—both written and practical. No special skills will be required of back of the house staff, but the proposal does recommend the hiring of a network administrator to manage the system and minimize down time.

"Well, I do have a lot to consider here! I start every new project with a SWOT analysis, and then check my references for relevant demographic/trend information. Paul is always makes sure that I have the most up-to-date demographics for any project he asks me to consider. I should have no problem making my decision before our Friday meeting."

First Quarter Forecasted Income Statement

Company Name	Internet Cafe		Brew Bucks
Sales			
Food Sales	$200,000		$ 222,000
Beverage Sales	$0		$87,000
Total Sales	**$200,000**		**$309,000**
Cost of Sales			
Food Cost	$70,000		$77,700
Beverage Cost	$0		$15,660
Total Costs	**$70,000**		**$93,360**
Gross Profit on Sales	**$130,000**		**$215,640**
Controllable Expenses			
Payroll	$40,000		$61,800
Employee Benefits	$8,000		$12,360
Direct Operating	$14,000		$21,630
Music & Entertainment	$6,000		$9,270
Repairs & Maintenance	$6,000		$9,270
Admin. & General	$14,000		$21,630
Advertising & Promotion	$10,000		$20,800
Utilities	$8,000		$12,360
Total Controllable Expenses	**$106,000**		**$169,120**
Profit before Occupation Costs	**$24,000**		**$46,520**
Occupation Costs			
Property Taxes	$2,423		$2,423
Rentals & Misc.	$400		$1,100
Liquor Lisc. Fees	$0		$1,450
Insurance	$4,102		$5,789
Lease Amortization	$1,200		$1,200
Interest—long term			
Depreciation	$6,380		$6,380
Total Occupation Costs	**$14,505**		**$18,342**
Other Income or Expense			
Extraordinary Income	$12,600		$9,000
Extraordinary Expense	$2,560		$3,100
Interest—Short Term			
Total Other Inc./Expense	**$10,040**		**$5,900**
Profit Before Taxes	**$19,535**		**$34,078**
Income Tax	**$6,447**		**$11,246**
Net Income (Loss)	**$13,088**		**$22,832**

4

Islip Schools Meet Gardetto's Food Service

Islip, New York -- Historically, school lunch programs existed for the purpose of ensuring underprivileged students at least one nutritionally balanced meal each day. Through the years, the programs have expanded to encompass breakfast, as well as afternoon snack programs, through the support of United States Department of Agriculture (USDA). Wholesomeness of the food has been the primary focus of the programs, while food quality has generally been a secondary concern. However, in the 1990s, school lunch programs are beginning to a different role in schools. School districts look to food service programs as a source of revenue. In many cases, these programs are required to generate income for the school corporation's operating budget.

School Board Meeting

The mood of the audience at the March School Board meeting in Islip, NY, could be described as hostile at best. This was the last of a series of public meetings held to discuss changes to the school meal program. As a direct result of budget cuts on federal, state, and local levels, the

Governor levied a two-million-dollar budget cut against the Islip School Corporation, effective for the July 1 operating budget. Given the socioeconomic mix, it is not anticipated that additional tax dollars will be able to make up the deficit in funding. The Islip school board, in the interest of maintaining all school programs at current levels, began to investigate options for cost cutting and/or revenue generation.

The school meal program has been a primary target of the finance investigation. The Director of School Food Service Operations, Eleanor Hall, has been with the district for over 28 years and director for 10 years. Among the ideas being investigated by the finance committee is whether or not the food service operations should take on a commercial franchise, use a management contractor, or remain an in-house food service operation. Mrs. Hall was appointed as head of the search committee which was seeking proposals from various contract food service management companies and quick service area franchisees. The School District felt that an outside contractor was necessary to develop a profitable food service component, as current programs are operating as efficiently as present practices allow.

After careful consideration, Gardetto's Food Service Company was selected as the best financial opportunity for the school district. It is believed that this contractor will be able to bring some of its subsidiaries, such as TACOS & MORE, PIZZAS, ETC., and/or BURGERS PLUS into the various cafeterias.

Irving Gardetto, President of Gardetto's Food Service, elected to make the presentation at the School board meeting himself. Although he was not normally inclined to make such presentations, he was aware of how potentially explosive the evening's meeting was likely to be. During the months that his company has been under consideration, there have been two well-organized groups actively working against the Gardetto's proposal. The group headed by PTA President, Meribeth Tasca, felt that the School District was "endangering our children's health and future intelligence in the UGLY name of profits." While the PTA group was vocal in its concerns, the outcry from the school food service workers was deafening. The majority of workers (65%) have been employed with the school corporation for eight years or more. They had become accustomed to job security, summers off, and generous benefit packages. The Gardetto's proposal called for the elimination of 20% of current non-union staffing positions, and for the remaining hourly union employees to be absorbed as Gardetto's employees. This would subject them to a reduction in health care benefits, a new and different retirement plan and integration into the Gardetto's seniority and compensation systems.

Joseph Micheletti, the Superintendent of Schools, was also apprehensive about this evening meeting. Mr. Micheletti moved from Florida to take the Islip Superintendent position 18 months ago, after the prior Superintendent was fired. His first few months on the job had been relatively uneventful, but the Governor's budget cuts had put an end to the "honeymoon" period. Since the announcement, Mr. Micheletti had been waging a daily battle to balance the needs and desires of the community with fiscal responsibility. It had seemed an impossible task until November, when Eleanor Hall sent him an article from the *Daily Pantagraph,* in Bloomington, Illinois, describing how that city's financial woes had been alleviated by turning over the operation of the school meal program to private industry.

After reading the article and speaking with the Superintendent of the Bloomington Schools, Mr. Micheletti met with Eleanor to begin exploring the possibility of implementing a similar program in Islip.

Together, they completed a comprehensive plan that called for a Request for Proposal (RFP) to be submitted to the district for the purpose of assuming management of the Islip school meal program. The qualifying proposals would be evaluated on predetermined criteria which would carefully balance nutritional soundness, consumer acceptance, and financial responsibility. As a means of balancing the motives of the management company with the responsibilities of the school system, the RFP specified that the position of Director of Food Service, currently held by Eleanor Hall, would remain a state employee, independent of the management company, but with supervising responsibilities. Of the RFPs evaluated, Gardetto's was selected as most meritorious and potentially appropriate for Islip. The plan to implement the Gardetto's proposal was announced at February School Board meeting and was received with mixed reactions.

The local press has been debating this issue for months and has further polarized the community. One local television station sided with the proposed changes, as a move toward cost savings and an end to government waste of tax dollars. However, another station focused on the concerns of parents and employees. They investigated other school systems served by Gardetto's, and found mixed results. Some communities and employees were happy with the change over and reported that the financial gains allowed their communities to continue arts and sports programs. One community reported that they were able to integrate computer education into all grade levels as a direct result of revenues generated.

Others were very unhappy with Gardetto's and were actively pursuing legal means of ending the contract. Some of the more inflammatory stories stated that the meals did not meet USDA nutritional guidelines, and despite promises of job security, two years after

Gardetto's had taken over the operation, 90% of former school system employees had been replaced by Gardetto's employees.

Mr. Micheletti watched as the auditorium filled. The room was fast approaching capacity and people were having difficulty finding seats. He watched Meribeth Tasca "working the room." Her camp was well organized and several members held posters with slogans such as "Stop Corporate Greed," "Burgers and Fries = Death," and "My Child's Future is Not for Sale!!!." Similarly, the employee's union had mobilized and were rallying behind signs that charged unfair labor practices.

Checking his watch, he realized that it was time for the meeting to begin. He reviewed his notes one last time, and then proceeded to the stage. Just before he went to the microphone, he mentioned to his administrative assistant that the audience microphone needed to be moved, since the number of people in the aisle would make access impossible. Mr. Micheletti cleared his throat and began the meeting.

"The school district has been faced with a major crisis; without changes we will need to cut 30–50% of our programs, with emphasis on sports and the band programs. As you may know, we had our finance committee investigate options and make recommendations for ways to cut costs and/or generate more revenue to pay for programs. The PTA has been very helpful, contributing over $35,000 this academic year.

"Our largest line item, next to payroll, has been the school meal program. Tonight, we will focus on a presentation detailing the already accepted proposal from Gardetto's Food Service. Please hold your questions until the end, and remember that we are all doing the best we can.

"Mr. Gardetto . . ."

Presentation by Mr. Gardetto

"The Islip school district has not had a history of long-term strategic planning, and these recent changes in the environment have put certain programs at risk. We at Gardetto's, propose to cut meal program costs by 80% and to work for a flat fee. We will return to the school budget 4% of the net profit on food service operations. This will be a large number of dollars because of the increased services we will create and manage. Please refer to the following slides for program information.

"I would be happy to answer any questions you have; please address just the information discussed."

Question #1 from Darren Davis, newspaper reporter

"What exactly do you have proposed for sports concessions?"

Response from Mr. Gardetto

"We plan to include provisions for the purchase a mobile kitchen setup for approximately $50,000 in the capital budget for the school district. We anticipate that by the end of the basketball season, it will have paid for itself and will be source of profit for the district."

Question #2 from a high school kitchen supervisor, Marian Marks

"I have a responsibility for guaranteeing the nutritional soundness of the food choices by students. All this sounds great, but how will you meet the USDA requirements? With all these fast food operations going into our schools—what kid wouldn't choose to have a burger or pizza over a spinach casserole?!"

Response from Mr. Gardetto

"We have three quick service operations, which we are able to include in our contract food service. We will analyze each junior high and high school program in the district, as well as sports concessions. Where the market will support these operations, we will put one or a combination of these three operations in that location. The elementary schools will served a six week cycle menu, with production coming from a central kitchen. The food will be transported in and served at each elementary school. This will include the breakfast and lunch programs."

Question #3 from Jacob Burns, parent

"Breyere Elementary has operated an on-site kitchen since the school opened in 1973. The meals have been good quality and my two boys have never been sick as a result of eating meals at their school. Your proposal calls for the closing of the Breyere school kitchen and for all the meals to be trucked in from a kitchen miles and miles way from the school. What guarantee can you give us that the meals won't poison my children with e. coli, Salmonella, or something worse?"

Response from Mr. Gardetto:

"Gardetto's has successfully implemented satellite kitchens in all of the systems for which we provide meals. In our entire history of school food service, we have never had an outbreak of food-borne illness attributed to Gardetto's handling of food products. Our standards for monitoring food quality and safety comply with, or exceed, industry standards. In addition, Eleanor Hall, who will be staying on as Director of Food Service for the district, will continue the training and education programs on Food Safety that she implemented two years ago. I am confident that you and your children will not notice any changes in the safety of the food served at the Breyere

School or, for that matter, at any school in the district. In fact we hope that you will see an improvement in the quality of food your children receive."

Question #4 from Jyala Sirapong, parent and teacher

"Islip is a diverse ethnic community with one-third of the school population having been in this country for less than five years. These students are often unfamiliar and uncomfortable with the language, customs, and foods of the American culture. In short, the typical cafeteria fare of hot dogs, sloppy joes, and grinders are at best unappealing, and at worst offensive to many of us non-Americans. What do you intend to do to serve this population?"

Response from Mr. Gardetto

"As part of our preliminary planning for Islip, we did a comprehensive study of the surrounding communities to examine the ethnicity, life-style, and economic make-up. Using this information, a 10-week Split Cycle menu was developed to consider the desires of diverse populations. Several revisions have been made to the original menus as a result of meetings with Eleanor Hall and representatives from the community, students, and parents. I believe we have come to a comprise that will please everyone. We intend to offer vegetarian options at every meal, and to incorporate ethnic specialties, as feasible, into the regular menu cycle."

Question #5 from Carolina Jenson, school food service worker

"I have worked for Islip schools for 20 years. We, my co-workers and I, are proud of what we do. We even have a motto "If you wouldn't serve it at home, don't serve it at here!" We are very proud of what we do.

We work real hard. We put are hearts into everything and...."

Mr. Michelletti, interrupts: —"Do you have a question, Mrs. Jenson?"

Carolina Jenson, school food service worker, continues—"Yes, I do. . . we are serious about feeding those students, Mr. Gardetto. How serious are you and your company? How will things change for us when the district sells out to your company?"

Response from Mr. Gardetto

"Let me start by saying that it saddens me to hear your refer to Gardetto's management of the school food service for Islip as a sell out. We at Gardetto's, view our involvement in contract food service as an critical merger of talents. We know food service, so we can use those talents to serve the school population. The school department knows education and teaching, and should be able to focus entirely on those endeavors. . . not wasting time worrying about school meals. That should be and will be our job. And let me clarify, when I say OUR—I mean ALL of us. We are successful in the area of school food service because we have been able to build partnerships between Gardetto's employees and School Department employees.

"That being said, employee input is critical to entire process, but the bottom line here is the 'bottom line.' We have to increase the number of non-reimbursable meals we serve. Customer counts must increase. So while we intend to involve new and old employees in the decision making process, the most critical information will come from our clients. We will be constantly evaluating the acceptance of our meals through surveys and observational evaluation methods. We all have to be willing to make changes to please and satisfy our clients."

Elliot Norwalk, Channel 5 reporter

"Mr. Gardetto's, I am a reporter for the Channel 5 evening news, but I am also the parent of four students enrolled in the Islip school system. I have had ample opportunity to review Gardettos' plans, and have no quarrels with the plan as written. Consideration was given to satisfy various constituencies in the community, and the savings for the city of $64,000 a year in employee benefits throughout the Gardetto's employment package is significant. The plan is comprehensive and well written.

"I am, however, concerned that historically in other districts that have moved to transfer the management of food operations to private companies, things have not turned out as well as planned. In fact, in almost all the school districts I have surveyed, the glowing forecast of profits never materialized. To make matters even worse, several districts are operating at substantial losses. I am concerned about the accuracy of your projections of meal counts and profits. Would you please clarify how they were arrived at, and what measures you will take to ensure that Islip does not suffer additional losses in the event your projections are not accurate?"

Response from Mr. Gardetto

"Good Evening, Mr. Norwalk. I am very familiar with your work. I was very impressed with the work you did on the "Taxpayer Rip-Offs—Now **you** KNOW" series. It was a great public service.

"With regard to our projections—we employed the data gathered from the community study, industry statistics, and Gardettos' history in similar markets to arrive at the projections presented. We believe that our company has a distinct advantage over our competition, because of our ability to provide well-known brand names—TACOS & MORE, PIZZAS, ETC. and BURGERS PLUS—in the school setting. We have established quarterly meetings with the school department and the superintendent to report on earnings and satisfaction. Furthermore. . ."

The Meeting Ends Abruptly

Mr. Micheletti stood up quickly, sensing Mr. Gardetto's discomfort with the question posed by Mr. Norwalk. "Ladies and Gentlemen, we thank you for your attention and questions this evening. I regret to end the meeting so abruptly, but with so many representatives from the press here this evening, we need to be sensitive to their needs to make the eleven p.m. news broadcasts. It is important that our whole community be informed. So once again, I thank you for your contributions this evening and Mr. Gardetto, thank you for personally taking the time to detail the plan. Let's hear a round of applause for Mr. Gardetto. . ." Mr. Micheletti hoped that the audience would follow his lead in applauding Mr. Gardetto. Several audience members began applauding weakly, but then they were drowned out by chanting and booing led by Meribeth Tasca.

2-Week Cycle Menu

Monday
Oven Chicken Nuggets
Dinner Roll
Oven Potatoes
Chilled Fruits
Milk

Tuesday
Breakfast or Lunch
French Toast w/ Syrup
or Scrambled Eggs
Cheese Sticks
Orange Juice
Fresh Apple
Milk

Wednesday
Spirals w/ Meat Sauce
Italian Bread
Garden Salad
Chilled Fruit
Milk

Thursday
Cold Cut Hoagie
Lettuce
Mustard
Fresh Fruit
Rice Pudding
Milk

Fabulous Friday
PIZZA, ETC. Day.
Peppy Pepperoni Pizza
Seasoned Crispy Bread
Salad
Ice Cream
Milk

Monday
Hamburger Delight
Rice
Lettuce and Tomato
Green Beans
Milk

Tuesday
Pork Cutlet on a Roll
Whipped Potatoes
Catsup
Chilled Fruit
Milk

Wednesday
Tuna Sandwich
Lettuce and Tomato
Potato Chips
Chilled Fruit
Milk

Terrific Thursday
BURGERS PLUS Day!
Irv's Burgers w/ Fixin' Buffet
French Fries
Cucumber Salad or Coleslaw
Milk

Friday
"Manager's Special"
Vegetable
Fruit
Milk

Monday
Food Long Hot Dogs
Beans
Chilled Fruit
Catsup
Milk

Tuesday
Grilled Cheese
  on White/ Wheat bread
Tater Puffs
Fruit Cocktails
Milk

Wonderful Wednesday
TACOS PLUS DAY!!!
Terrific Tacos w/ Salsa
Corn
Jell-O w/ Whipped Topping
Milk

Thursday
Fried Rice w/ Egg Roll
Italian Bread
Fruit
Milk

Friday
Fish & Cheese on a Roll
Fresh Coleslaw
Potato Chips
Chilled fruit
Milk

Food and Beverage Operations

Annual Budget Forecast

Islip Schools - Gardetto's Food Service Co.		
Sales		
Contract Sales	$6,318,000.00	72.00%
Cash Cafeteria	$1,316,250.00	15.00%
Faculty/ Staff Sales	$263,250.00	3.00%
Catering & Concessions	$877,500.00	10.00%
Total Sales	**$8,775,000.00**	**100.00%**
Cost of Sales		
Food	$3,948,750.00	45.00%
Gross Profit	**$4,826,250.00**	**55.00%**
Labor Costs		
Management	$263,250.00	3.00%
Payroll	$2,106,000.00	24.00%
Employee Benefits	$243,067.50	2.77%
Operating Expenses		
Paper Goods	$175,500.00	2.00%
Cleaning Supplies	$43,875.00	0.50%
Linen and Laundry	$87,750.00	1.00%
Replacements	$74,587.50	0.85%
Insurance	$109,687.50	1.25%
Repair & Maintenance	$175,500.00	2.00%
Trash Removal	$67,567.50	0.77%
Misc. Charges	$307,125.00	3.50%
Total Operating Expenses	**$3,015,967.50**	**34.37%**
Net Operating Profit	**$1,810,282.50**	**20.63%**
Occupation Costs		
Commissions/ Rent	$284,000.00	3.24%
Depreciation	$100,000.00	8.50%
Amortization	$200,000.00	2.28%
Other Charges	$194,600.00	2.22%
Total Occup. Costs	**$778,600.00**	**8.87%**
Net Profit	**$1,031,682.50**	**11.76%**

Islip Schools - Gardetto'sGardetto's Food Service Co.

Sales		
Food		80.00%
Beverage		20.00%
Total Sales	**$1,000,000.00**	100.00%
Cost of Sales		
Food		37.50%
Beverage		27.50%
Total Cost of Sales		
Gross Profit		
Controllable Expenses		
Payroll		28.00%
Employee Benefits		4.25%
Direct Operating Expenses		4.50%
Music and Entertainment		0.50%
Advertising and Promotion		1.50%
Utilities		2.75%
Administration & General		3.00%
Repair & Maintenance		1.50%
Tot. Controllable Expenses		46.00%
Income Before Occupation Costs		
Occupation Costs		
Rent	$55,000.00	
Property Taxes	$5,500.00	
Other Taxes	$4,500.00	
Property Insurance	$15,000.00	
Interest	$12,500.00	
Depreciation	$22,500.00	
Tot. Occup. Costs	$115,000.00	
Restaurant Profit BeforeTaxes		

SENESAC HOTEL

Hastings, Pennsylvania

A Letter Arrives

398 Blackstone Boulevard
Providence, RI 02906
September 5, 1996

Mrs. Leona Senesac, Owner
Senesac Hotel Corporation
2354 Heron Drive
West Lafayette, IN 47096

Dear Mrs. Senesac:

I have stayed at the Senesac Hotel on numerous occasions when on business, and have always enjoyed the service and amenities immensely. Unfortunately, my last stay at the hotel, 2 weeks ago, was not at all pleasant. Despite numerous attempts to have management resolve the difficulties I was experiencing, <u>nothing</u> was addressed to my satisfaction. I am writing this letter to you in the hope that you will personally address my concerns and provide me with assurances that these issues have been resolved. Otherwise, you can be guaranteed that I will secure alternative accommodations the next time I stay in the Hastings, Pennsylvania, area.

My "adventure" at the Senesac Hotel began at check-in. As I entered the lobby of the hotel, I was nearly overcome by the aroma of fried food laced with chlorine. The property was obviously having a ventilation problem in both the kitchen and the pool area. I approached the front desk, which was staffed by only one desk clerk on a Friday night, and waited to be served. I stood at the desk for a full 10 minutes before my presence was acknowledged, and then rather than waiting on me, the clerk bellowed to someone in the back that he was "in the weeds."

The person who emerged from the back office was evidently some kind of manager, as he was dressed in a suit rather than a uniform. His first words to me were to request my credit card—NOT "Good Evening," NOT "How may I help you?" but "I need to see your credit card". Taken aback, I handed him my card. He strolled halfway over to the computer before he turned back to ask "What's your name?" I responded, "Its on the card". That information provided, he proceeded to check me in. I commented to him that I had tried to call the hotel earlier to verify several details I had arranged, and that I was put on hold for at least 10 minutes at premium long-distance rates. The "manager's" response was "Well, we've been really busy today." The check-in procedure completed, he handed me my key card, returned my credit card,." and walked away. My request for directions to my room was answered, but with a definite tone of annoyance.

I found my room with little difficulty, but opening the door was another ordeal. The directions provided on the door handle and the ones on the key varied significantly. After several attempts, I found that a combination of steps outlined by both the door and key, as well as a fair amount of forceful language, was sufficient to open the door. I was surprised to find that the room was not only exceedingly dark, due to numerous burned out light bulbs, but was also very hot. A quick check of the thermostat revealed that the room was a balmy 92 degrees.

The heat in the room prompted my first phone call to front desk. That call was answered after 12 rings and I was told to "put the air conditioning on high and go out for a walk." Unfortunately, this was not an option for me as I was anticipating a very important business call and had elected to order room service. Thankfully, although delivery was not as timely as I would have liked, the meal itself was delightful. I began to hope that this was a turning point in my stay.

However, at 2:30 a.m., I was awakened by a brisk knock at my door. I staggered to the door and opened it. Standing before me was a disheveled Bellperson who demanded to know if he had left a yellow bag in my room. (Yellow is not my color.) I reminded him that he had not assisted me with my luggage. He turned and walked away mumbling something about the wrong room. I returned to bed and attempted to fall back to sleep. At 4:00 a.m., I was awakened by a wrong number wake-up call and I decided once again to call the front desk. This time the phone was answered after 10 rings. I requested the name of the General Manager, and was informed that his name was Mr. Wickfielden, but they were unsure of how to spell his name. As a result of this experience, I chose to write to you directly. I did however find it interesting that no one was concerned that I might be having a problem when I requested the manager's name.

I called the front desk and asked not to be disturbed for the rest of the day. I also hung out the "do not disturb sign" which communicates this in five different languages. Promptly at 8:00 a.m., there was a knock on the door—this time from housekeeping, asking what time I was planning to check out. I wanted to check out immediately, but when I called my secretary to ask her to make other hotel arrangements <u>quickly</u> , the local area hotels were all sold out. I kept telling myself that I have stayed here for years, and this must all be a fluke. While I was in the shower, a violent siren went off—I assumed it was the fire alarm, so I grabbed my laptop computer and a towel as I rushed out of my room to the stairwell and down 10 flights of stairs. The siren still blaring, I arrived in the lobby, to find everyone going about their normal business. It seems it was a scheduled check of the fire alarm system. Needless to say, I was not pleased to be standing in the lobby with only a towel on, even if I do have a great body. The front desk clerk walked me to a service elevator and let me back into my room.

About an hour later, I received from the management the first in an installment of seven fruit baskets that I was to receive during my stay. Please note that the last two baskets were accompanied by bottles of wine. While I am not in the produce business, I definitely had enough fruit to open my own stand.

I already had reservations in the dining room, so I decided to keep these arrangements, since the food has always been consistently excellent. My third fruit basket arrived as a result of my dinner experience. The chicken was raw and bloody. My guests were very shaken when seeing this and refused to finish eating. I escorted my guests to a cab, and returned to take the issue up with the manager. By the time I returned 10 minutes later, they had cleared our plates and charged the meals to my room. I spoke with the dining room manager who said she would take care of everything and remove the dinner from my bill. However, upon check-out I found the meals still charged to my guest bill.

My last evening in the hotel, I called down for an early wake-up call. Ten minutes later the phone rang; it was the attendant calling to ask again what time I wanted the call. The wake-up call, however, never came. As a result, I was late in waking up and nearly missed my plane. My departure from your hotel was further complicated, when I became "trapped" in the elevator with a bride on her way to her room—her long train got stuck in the door and she began to cry hysterically. By this point I just wanted out of your hotel. Frustrated, I nevertheless paid my bill and then asked for assistance with my luggage. The clerk paged the Bellperson, who entered the lobby SINGING "Oh, What a Beautiful Morning" at the top of his lungs.

I was deeply disturbed by my stay. I serve people everyday in my practice and I know the importance of listening to them. I hope that you will provide me with assurance that you have addressed these issues.

Sincerely,

Augustus Macillia, M.D.

Mrs. Senesac's Response

Mrs. Senesac sat back in her chair, rubbed her eyes, and summoned Chad, her personal assistant, telling him to bring her a double. This was her way of letting him know that there was an important matter to be addressed and that she was not pleased. Mrs. Senesac handed Chad the letter and gave him a moment to read it. When he had finished reading the letter, she instructed him to call Hastings IMMEDIATELY and have the following items faxed to her directly:

1. Dr. Macillia's guest history information.

2. The guest folio from Dr. Macillia's recent stay.

3. Full copies of manager and desk log from the week of Dr. Macillia's stay.

4. Incident reports related to Dr. Macillia's experiences.

5. The names of all personnel known to have had contact with Dr. Macillia.

She also instructed Chad to fax the letter to Eric Wickford, General Manager of the Hastings property, and indicate that she required a personal response back by the end of the day.

The information requested arrived quickly and upon surveying it, Mrs. Senesac gleaned the following information: She found that hotel had indeed been scheduled for the annual fire alarm test during Dr. Macillia's stay; however the corporate policy of guest notification had not occurred. In addition, she discovered that the following managers had independently elected to send fruit baskets to the distressed guest—the Front Desk Supervisor, the Executive Housekeeper, the Food and Beverage Manager, the Dining Room Manager, and the Bell Captain. The General Manager was more generous, sending two fruit baskets, complete with wine, one of which was delivered to Dr. Macillia's home. Nowhere, in all of the documentation, could she find evidence that the issues had been resolved in any manner other than the "fruit basket approach." This concerned Mrs. Senesac deeply, as Dr. Macillia's stays with the hotel in the previous year had accounted for 21 room nights and his least expensive folio charge was $700.00.

Dissatisfied with the information provided by the reports, Mrs. Senesac anxiously anticipated Mr. Wickford's response. At 4:30 p.m., Chad brought Mrs. Senesac a cup of chamomile tea with honey, and Mr. Wickford's letter, hot off the fax machine.

To: Leona Senesac

From: Eric Wickford

Date: September 9, 1995

Re: The Macillia Letter

Thank you for your fax this morning. First of all, I want to assure you that we will do everything in our power to resolve these issues immediately. I truly appreciate and understand your concerns. I would, however, like to take this opportunity to inform you that I was on vacation during the time of Dr. Macillia's stay and it was my secretary Bianca who took it upon herself to authorize the fruit baskets and sign my name to the card. I have dealt with her accordingly, and she assures me that she will feel less empowered in the future.

In the interest of clarity, I will address the concerns of the letter in chronological order. Michael Goldstein was the desk manager on duty the night in question, and did indeed check in the guest. However, his communication skills were impaired, due to a double root canal he had earlier in the day. He has volunteered to write a letter of apology to Dr. Macillia and will supply documentation, if requested. He was not at the desk when Dr. Macillia approached because he was attempting to contact Gilbert Ventilation, regarding the aromas that were filling the lobby. This problem has since been fixed. The repairs were not covered by warrantee, and I will be sending you more information regarding that issue later. By the way, Michael has consistently earned high performance marks, was Employee of the Month in August, and is being considered for a promotion.

The room key issue was a result of the transition to ECO-Key program, as mandated by the Senesac Corporation. The entire change over has now been completed and only one set of directions exists. Quite frankly, I am amazed that he was able to open the door at all! The heat in the room was related to the ventilation problem that I referred to earlier, and as I pointed out, has since been resolved.

I have been unable to get to bottom of the bellperson and wake-up call issues. The bellperson responsible for the incident was fired 2 days ago for a no-show/no-call. Incidentally, this is the same singing bellperson referred to later in the letter. With regard to the 4:00 a.m. wake-up call, the phone logs have no record of calls made to the room in question at that hour, for any of the days of his stay. There is a note in the log, however, that room 1024 called at 4:10 a.m. on August 23. The guest was irate, screamed foul language at the operator, and demanded my name! She was shaken, as this was her third night as an employee at the Senesac, and as a result, scrambled my name. She has been spoken to about this and understands that she may not make this type of error in the future.

There is a note in the desk log that at 8:30 a.m., housekeeping disturbed a guest on the 10th floor. Unfortunately, the exact room number was not noted. I suppose it is safe to assume that Dr. Macillia was the guest awakened. As an gesture of goodwill, Paul Shermis, our executive housekeeper, sent every stay-over room on the floor a fruit basket.

The next complaint in the letter addressed the fire alarm testing. I agree that this was an unfortunate event. As I stated earlier, I was on vacation during the time of these incidents, and as a result, the customary guest notification letters required by corporate, were not distributed to guests at check-in. This oversight was discovered at 9:00 a.m. and immediately voice messages were left for all guests on the telephone system. This was signaled to guests by the light flashing on the telephone unit. If Dr. Macillia had only noticed this, the incident would never have occurred. However, I have to be frank and question why he continued to the lobby, when he noticed that he was the only one in the stairwell!! I am thankful that the desk staff had the foresight to escort him to his room via the service elevator. In addition, I am further investigating why Security allowed a semi-nude man to progress to the lobby, given the plethora of security cameras we recently installed, per corporate's requirements.

I have spoken with Mike Toohill regarding the bloody chicken served to 8 guests on the date in question. It seems that in this case, Dr. Macillia was not the <u>only</u> guest effected. All meals involved were completely compensated.

In regard to the wake-up call, Bianca had instructed all staff members to double check all Dr. Macillia's requests to ensure that they were addressed appropriately, given his track record of complaints. The phone call made to as a follow-up to Dr. Macillia's wake-up call request was not as a result of staff incompetence, but rather an attempted to verify they had the correct details. Phone log records indicate that an automated wake-up call was placed and answered in Dr. Macillia's room at 5:00 a.m. As a result, his delayed departure from the hotel was not our fault.

Finally, the elevator incident has been blown out of proportion. The bride, who was still a bit tipsy from the previous night, accidentally stumbled into the elevator thinking it was her room. Her tears stemmed from her disappointment at finding a rather mature gentleman with her, rather than her groom. The elevator was stalled for a grand total of 7 minutes. Hardly a length of time to be so upset about.

Please keep me posted on your progress with resolving these issues. As I stated earlier, we are doing everything possible at our end to address the issues within our control.

Background

Present-day setting is a medium-sized hotel in the metropolitan area of Hastings, Pennsylvania, with an interstate exit access of less than a half a mile. Hastings is a suburb of Philadelphia, approximately eight miles from the Philadelphia Airport. Leona Senesac, is an absentee owner, residing in the Midwest to be closer to her grandchildren.

The Senesac Hotel, built in 1983, is four stories tall with a large glass atrium A detached parking garage is adjacent to the hotel and is free to patrons staying more than two nights. The White Elm Room, which is located in the lobby, has seating for 80 people and does a heavy breakfast business. A lunch and dinner menu is also offered. The restaurant primarily serves hotel guests. Hours are 6:00 a.m. to 9:30 a.m. for breakfast, 11:00 a.m. to 2:00 p.m. for lunch and 5:00 p.m.- 11:00 p.m. for dinner. Room service offers a limited selection, and uses a different menu from that of the White Elm Room. Room service hours are 6:30 a.m. until 11:00 p.m. Three function rooms and two conference rooms are also available through the Sales and Catering office. Sales and Catering is open Monday through Friday from 9:00 a.m. to 6:00 p.m. and from 9:00 a.m. to 1:00 p.m.on Saturday.

Management

An executive operating committee (EOC) oversees key decisions in the hotel. The committee is comprised of the management team including: Eric Wickford, General Manager; Lucy Hall, Resident Manager; Mike Toohill. Food and Beverage Manager;

Georgia Mayfield, Human Relations Manager; Chris Rutledge. Rooms Division Manager, and Melvin Wagner, Director of Sales and Catering.

Eric Wickford has been the General Manager for the five years Mrs. Senesac has owned the hotel. Prior to his current position, he held a previous management position in the Boston area. Eric is 57 years old and after his last physical, required by the company, was told to "get more exercise." He has a B.S. degree in business from Penn State, and has been married to Martha, a domestic engineer, for thirty-five years. Eric and Martha have six children, two of whom are now employed in the hospitality field.

Lucy Hall is the Resident Manager, age 27, and has been with the Senesac Hotel for six months. In her previous job, she worked in Florida as a rooms division manager in a small hotel of a major domestic corporation. Lucy's Master's Degree in Hospitality is from UNLV, where she also worked as a teaching assistant.

Mike Toohill has been with the company for almost five years as Food and Beverage Manager, and has a degree in business from Penn State. Mike is divorced, 55 years old, and is known as a hard worker. Mr. Toohill has been working on a plan to reposition the White Elm Restaurant in the market. The executive chef transferred from another Senesac property and is not supportive of Mr. Toohill's ideas for the restaurant.

Georgia Mayfield, 32, is the new Human Relations Director, a new position in the Senesac Hotel. Management felt this position was needed as the number of employees continues to increase. Additionally, the demands of ADA regulations and other legislation has justified this position. On several occasions, Ms. Mayfield has been late for work because of car accidents. Georgia is due for her annual review; her six month performance review was disappointing.

Chris Rutledge, the Rooms Division Manager, is 35 years old and a graduate of "The School of Hard Knocks." Although Chris has no formal education in the hospitality field, he has made a good transition from his first position as a housekeeper. Chris' department has the lowest turnover of any department in the hotel.

Melvin Wagner is the Director of Engineering and Maintenance, and has no formal education beyond high school. He has been with the property for three years, and Mrs. Senesac gave him his first job. He is 44 years old , has been divorced twice, and is now remarried. He has eight children, three of whom are preschool age and live with him now. His wife is going to school full-time at Penn State to obtain a BS degree in nursing.

Marketing Position

The Senesac Hotel is primarily targeted toward the business traveler, with some seasonal holiday business centered around the leisure traveler. Function business is from the local industries who need training and/or meeting facilities. The room mix includes: 15% Suites with separate sitting and sleeping rooms, including a whirlpool bath and wet bar; 85% Comfort rooms which are slightly smaller than the Suites and have only a wet bar. The average rack rate for the 300 room hotel is $135.00.

Hotel occupancy has been 73%. Food and Beverage operations (48% of total sales) have long been considered a primary revenue source for the hotel's income statement. Local businesses have some interest in off -premise catering. The hotel has a swimming pool and provides shuttle service within a ten-mile radius.

6

WATERBURY INN

Waterbury, CT

Background

Dr. Brown was always looking for a "good investment." He tended to follow the crowd in this pursuit. If securities were recommended at the club, securities were what he bought. When silver was the "sure bet," he bought precious metals.

In 1988, at the height of the real estate market, Dr. Brown began to explore opportunities in this arena. He was especially interested in the concept of a bed and breakfast operation in a historic building. He believed this would provide him with notoriety, a steady income, and best of all a quick return on his investment. He also believed it would be easy to keep the cost of operation low. After all, such get-aways were now the "in-thing."

Dr. Brown believed that utility and repair costs would be very low because guests wouldn't be living there, but would only be staying a few days. He also intended to enforce strict screening policies for all potential guests. His location would be popular, so he felt he could afford to be choosy. Air conditioning would be undesirable because it would disturb the integrity of the theme. Likewise, heating costs could be substantially reduced by providing guests with down quilts and old-fashioned bed warmers.

After a long and arduous search, Dr. Brown settled on what he believed to be the ideal property. The mansion that was to become the Waterbury Inn is located on two acres of land in an affluent suburb. The mansion stands at the top of a long circular driveway, and features a carriage port and sprawling open-air porch. The 30-room home had been majestically planned to include a grand central stairway, the focal point of the large entry hall. Located on the first floor were two large sitting rooms, a grand dining room and a smaller family/ billiard room. The kitchen, also located on the first floor, is connected to the main house by a serving pantry.

Bedrooms are located on the second and third floors of the house. Each floor has eight bedrooms and five full baths. The fourth floor is comprised of what were the living quarters for the serving staff. The main stairwell of the house provides access to the first, second and third floors. The fourth floor can only be accessed by the back stairs in the kitchen. These stairs allow access to all the floors of the house, including the basement.

Dr. Brown purchased the property for $2 million dollars. The final price for the distressed property was reached after several months of negotiation with the owners of the estate. Following the closing, Dr. Brown hired Hospitality, Inc., an industry consulting firm, to oversee the renovation of the property.

Alicia O'Neill founded the firm in November of 1984. She and her husband John are devoted to the hospitality industry and have both worked in the field for a number of years. Alicia's expertise lies primarily in Human Resource Management, Consumer Behavior and Interior Design/Landscaping. John has strengths in finance, procedures and industry trends. Together the are a powerful team.

After inspecting the property carefully, Hospitality Inc., presented Dr. Brown with a plan for renovation that would require a $1.5 million investment for interior work, furnishings and decoration. This would be enhanced by an additional $1 million dollars spent on landscaping and the addition of a gazebo in the garden. Renovations would focus on developing the second and third floors as guest rooms and the fourth floor as living quarters for the Inn's caretakers. Plans for the first floor included renovating the second sitting room as a library, and creating a nursery/ playroom environment in the old billiard room.

The entire renovation project took 9 months to complete. The Waterbury Inn opened its doors to guests in September of 1993. The rooms were exquisitely appointed with period pieces and replicas appropriate to the Victorian Era home. There are four King rooms (two on each floor), each with private baths; eight Queen rooms (four on each floor), with shared bathrooms, and four Full rooms (two on each floor), that also have one twin size bed and have shared baths.

The dining room serves continental style breakfast Monday through Friday between the hours of 6:30 a.m. and 9:00 a.m. More substantial fare is served on Saturday, Sunday, and Mondays of holiday weekends. Guests can make arrangements for evening meals when 24 hours notice is given to the Inn staff.

Early on, Dr. Brown made it very clear that he intended to have very little involvement in the operation of the property. His interest was in his return on investment. As a result, a young couple, Jill and Russell Stephens, were employed as caretakers of the Waterbury Inn. The couple were new to the area and had one child. Russell holds a Master's Degree in

Public Policy from a local university, and Jill, although certified as a secondary school teacher, has chosen to stay at home as the primary caregiver for their child. The Stephens were delighted at the opportunity to manage the Waterbury Inn, as it would allow them to live in a "good community" and would substantially cut their living expenses. To round out the staff at the Waterbury Inn, a local woman was hired to provide cleaning services, and a retired baker was hired to prepare pastries daily.

The Waterbury Inn's occupancy averages around 8% with the exception of certain weekends associated with activities at the local universities and colleges, including parents weekends, graduation, or university homecoming. Occupancy during these weekends has been 100% for two day stays. The room rates are $110- $150 a night. The Inn has a AAA membership, but few guests select the Waterbury Inn due to promotions of the AAA. Three months after the grand opening, the Stephens' ran an advertisement in *The New York Times* for 13 weeks. This resulted in a grand total of two clients.

Recent Changes

Several changes have occurred at the Waterbury Inn in the past three years. The Stephens' are expecting twins in the next four months which will bring the family total to five. Jill has had a difficult pregnancy. and has been confined to bed 15 hours a day, with strict instructions to avoid all possible strain. Russell has taken a position as an adjunct professor with a local college to help make ends meet. As a result, the Stephens' have had limited time to devote to the operation, and have hired a college student to manage front desk operations.

Kerry Kemper is a junior at the University of New Haven and anticipates receiving her Bachelor's degree in Hospitality Administration within the next 18 months. She answered the advertisement placed in the local paper, and after meeting with Dr. Brown and the Stephens', accepted a two-year position at the Waterbury. In exchange for room and board, Kerry would oversee the front desk, billing, and reservations. Russell would continue to oversee the kitchen and housekeeping functions, and Jill, who was becoming bedridden, would concentrate on keeping reports flowing to Dr. Brown via her laptop computer.

Kerry moved into the fourth floor caretaker quarters, while the Stephens' moved to the second floor and took over three of the rooms—one king room, and two of the full/twin rooms. This reduced the number of available guest rooms to 13. The move was required because Jill could no longer climb the stairs to the fourth floor.

For the first three months, operations at the Waterbury ran without incident. The occupancy was running at its traditionally low rate, but they were headed into the spring season, a time that usually resulted in increased occupancy. Kerry used the Waterbury Inn as the subject of a marketing class project, and had developed a brochure highlighting the beautiful landscaping of the property. She had this brochure mass produced and mailed to all past guests of the property. This generated 38 additional reservations during the months of April and May.

On April 29, Dr. Brown received an urgent phone call from Kerry. It was not customary for Kerry to communicate directly with him, as Jill was responsible for reporting functions. Nonetheless, Dr. Brown took the call and was very disturbed by the information she relayed. Kerry explained that she was calling from campus and that she was very concerned about what she had seen at the Waterbury over the weekend. On Friday night, a single man checked into the Waterbury, He was a walk-in guest, but provided a gold credit card as means of payment. He requested a room with as much privacy as possible and was given a room on the third floor. He registered as a party of two in the registration book, stayed one night, and checked out of the Inn without incident.

At about 10:00 a.m., when Mrs. Sims went to clean the room, she began shouting about the condition of the room. She stormed down the stairs and demanded that someone else take care of it. Kerry and Russell went to the room and found that the sheets were stained heavily with blood and feces. Several towels in the bathroom were similarly stained, and there were used condoms in the sink and trash. Russell turned and left the room. He went downstairs and told Mrs. Sims that he would pay her an extra $50.00 to clean the room. She asked for gloves, but Russell told her that she didn't need them. No one like that would ever stay at the Waterbury.

Kerry was very concerned that basic precautions had been ignored, and threatened to quit. Dr. Brown assured her that he would take appropriate action immediately and made a note to call the Stephens' as soon as possible. His call to the Stephens' was disturbing. Russell was off property and Jill could not tell him expected reservations for the week. Her due date was a month away, and it seemed that she had not left the second floor in three weeks. This deeply concerned Dr. Brown, as it appeared that no one was managing his investment. With Kerry and Russell both off property, there was no one managing the front desk. He determined it was time for action.

Dr. Edward Brown contacted Hospitality, Inc., once again. He explained his situation and his concerns that his investment was not paying off. He had been advised that he could recover his investment within seven years. At present, Dr. Brown had not seen any indication that this was going to occur, and was very concerned, the Waterbury Inn was only adding additional liability to his financial portfolio. Alicia was unavailable at the present time and John was out on a consulting job, but a new associate, Michael Johns, was available immediately. They made arrangements for Michael to make a "secret shopper" property inspection of the Waterbury within the week.

Hospitality, Inc.

THE EXPERTS IN ACCOMMODATIONS.
YOU HAVE A FRIEND IN THE INDUSTRY.

Report submitted by: Michael Johns, Associate in Hospitality
Property: Waterbury Inn, Waterbury, Connecticut.

Thursday stay—Reservations made 48 hours in advance

Phone Reservations - Through AAA—no knowledge of this
property—rating has lapsed.

Called directly, pleasant and guaranteed with credit card

Check In - Early check in (2 p.m.)—told the room was ready
and shown to a 2nd floor room 208.

Room Condition - Tidy, well lit, mix of contemporary
furniture with antique reproductions, stale, dusty, and musty.
Dark hair on the pillow case, message light would not go off,
walls not sound proof—could hear crying baby most of the
night.

Staff - pleasant and helpful

Breakfast - Advertising "homemade." but a BROSHES
Bakery truck delivered a box at 5:30 a.m. I stayed for all three
serving hours—noted no other guests, when asked, no other
guests staying. Coffee was cold because the coffee pot was not
heated.

Property Overall - trash in the parking lot, poor driving
directions with distances off. Missing clear signage.

Checkout - manual checkout, lost my original credit card
voucher, about 11 minutes to check out.

Follow-Up - Returned to pick up watch left behind. Front
desk clerk, Kerry Kemper, discussed freely her frustration
with the property. Concern over safety and sanitation
handling of bloody sheets, concern over lack of marketing,
openly discussed that no one other than herself has any
hospitality training. Reports they are lucky to sell "a room a
night."

Recommendation - discuss this property, in person continue
the surprise shopping.

Memo

To: Alicia O'Neill
From: Michael Johns
Date: June 12, 1995
Subject: Waterbury Inn

Please find attached my secret shopper's report as requested. I have the following concerns I believe require further investigation:

1. Number of rooms occupied by family members

2. Housekeeping cleaning procedures

3. The actual breakfast menu and the claims of being "homemade"

4. Cash control procedures

5. AAA rating claims—the sign is still on the door

6. There appears to be a couple of competing properties which are similar, and listed with AAA: TheRed Cabin House and The Country Herb Inn.

The Economy

There are several hotels in close proximity to the Waterbury Inn. The metropolitan area of New Haven has an average occupancy of 52%, with downtown rates in the range of $75-$250. There are also plans for a Convention Center to be built in the downtown area. The only competition is the area is The Red Cabin House. The Red Cabin House is the only other bed and breakfast in town and is located three miles away from the Waterbury Inn. The Red Cabin House has the majority of its 12 rooms filled on a regular basis by the repeat customers. The Innkeeper describes her operation as a "friendly stay in an old Victorian home". It is furnished completely in antiques, and the employees wear clothing from the period.

The New England area is in the second year of a declining economy. The nearby state of Rhode Island had a banking crisis involving credit unions which were not federally insured. Over 40 credit unions in the immediate area closed on January 1, 1991.

Industry observers saw 1990 as a year of status quo operations. The gulf crisis in Middle East, which began in August of 1990; the scare of terrorism and the activation of 300,000 troops in the Reserves contributed to a conservative approach by government and individuals. Gasoline prices increased $.35 to .45 during the Desert Shield Military action. During this time, travelers were more likely to choose destinations closer to home due to increases in gas prices and international safety issues.

Market Segment

Hospitality, Inc., determined that the Waterbury Inn has two types of guests. One type is the parents who come in three times a year for the local university events. The second type of guest is the business traveler. They described the business persons who stays in the inn as those who want a clean, friendly environment.

Hospitality, Inc., recommended that the Waterbury go after the business traveler as the primary guest. Local businesses have a frequent need for accommodations for out-of-town employees attending local training functions. This approach would require additional investment which Dr. Brown says he cannot afford. Dr. Brown believes that the $250.00 he spent on the sign for the Waterbury Inn is a good enough investment in advertising.

The Stephens' seem unsure how to set room rates. The money arrangements are summarized as "making it," for another six months. The mortgage is a 30-year loan at 11%. They also have a short-term loan at 15%

for the amount of the renovation. Operating costs, not including the mortgage, are around $100,000 a year. Currently the owners are not taking a salary. Some creditors are making third calls on requests for payments. The hotel suppliers of the bed linens and pillows are threatening them with criminal proceedings.

## 7

UP THE "INTERNET" WITHOUT THE MANUAL

BlueLakes Corporation

Peter and Rose Eder have held their
BlueLakes Inn Motel franchise for the
past 10 years. They purchased it upon
Peter Eder's retirement at the age of 62.
Peter was a boiler maintenance engineer
for a major Wisconsin insurance firm for
36 years. In planning for their retirement
years, the couple had determined that
they wanted to establish a business
together that would allow them to work
side by side, but at the same time would
not be so demanding that they would not
be able to relax and travel.

It was Rose who found the lead on the
BlueLakes Inn Motel franchise. The
company had taken a unique approach to
property management, preferring to sell
franchises to older, but active couples,
who would be committed to staying with
the property for a number of years. In
addition, corporate guaranteed
franchisees two weeks off per year.
During this two-week vacation period,
operation of the property would be
covered by college students employed
and trained by corporate. Revenue figures
related to the Franchise agreement were
also impressive. Royalty fees are 5% of

total revenue and advertising/promotion rates are figured at 1.5% of total revenues. Computer equipment and furnishings are available at cost or at a profound discount rate. In addition, part of Rose's interest in BlueLakes Inns focused on its well-developed reservations system. As a result, Peter and Rose decided to actively review the available properties which corporate had to offer.

Rose and Peter chose a BlueLakes Inn property with 88 rooms, which had been newly constructed outside of Wichita Falls, at the intersection of Interstate 44 and highway 287 in Texas. The Wichita Falls property was less than three years old when it was purchased by Pete and Rose. Some competition has sprung up on the interstate at a prior exit, with corporate properties such as Mariott Courtyards and Holiday Inn Express charging rack rates between $89.00 and $129.00 a night. The BlueLakes Inn was running with a rack rate of $49.00 to $59.00, depending on the type of room. The BlueLakes Inn has no function rooms, and for meals, usually recommends Beningo's, a family restaurant a quarter mile down the road.

Over the years, occupancy has been good, ranging from 79% to 81%. There is a steady group of repeat customers who come in for fairs and shows at the local expo-center. Historically, Rose and Pete Eder have taken their vacation the last two weeks in July. Their travel has always been out of the region and back to Milwaukee to visit friends and see the sights. The Eders usually take a driving trip, flying out of Milwaukee if they take any side trips.

Background

BlueLakes Corporation was established in 1979, in Midland, Michigan. A group of retired executives from Dow Chemical chose to take on second careers in Hotel Operations. The energy crisis was over, and people were beginning to do more traveling. This influenced them to set up a company where franchisees could buy property with the market research already completed. As proof of the revenue possibilities, the corporation would own and operate new properties for the first two to three years, until the operation was well entrenched. To date, there are 17 franchisees, with the average operator owning two properties throughout the Midwest. The name of the company was the result of a fishing trip taken by Raymond Hughes and John Zellers. Both men are now in their 70s and are active in the corporate operations. The corporate leaders are looking for someone to buy them out over the next five years. Hughes and Zellers took on Marie Tremblay, a new Dow retiree, formerly the Technology Vice President of Plant Operations in North America

Marie is interested in making sure that the franchise agreements are periodically reviewed. She has placed emphasis on ensuring that franchisees are offered the technology and training support needed to increase revenues. There have not been any lawsuits from any franchisees. It seems that the "benefit" package has been the key selling point with new franchisees. The BlueLakes Corporate office is one of the few offices operating with minimal layers of executives. The operation is simple. yet sophisticated. Thanks to the fax machine and e-mail links, communication has greatly improved.

The Wichita Falls BlueLakes property has been sold out over 120 nights per year since it has been in operation. Additionally, it has 40% of its business from repeat high school sports groups. The physical plant is still in "mint" condition because of the quality construction and decorating completed at the time of building the motel. Overall, the demand for rooms was increasing in the community with the area occupancy rate at 78%. This region has not been subject to seasonal fluctuations.

The Eders employ a total of five staff members. In addition to Jim, there are three housekeepers—one head housekeeper and 2 maids, and Maxine O'Keefe, who works part time as a desk clerk. This core staff is supplemented as needed by a handyman who does repairs and upkeep for the property on a casual labor basis.

The day of Eileen's arrival, Peter and Rose started their day as they always did, by having coffee with Jim Rodrigues, the night desk clerk. Jim works six days a week from 10:00 p.m. to 6:00 a.m., and has been an employee of the Eders for the past seven years. Each morning at 5:00 a.m., the Eders met with Jim as a means of shift transition. They then proceeded to complete various night audit functions, room assignments, and the housekeeper's report.

As she began her day, Rose reread the letter of introduction sent from corporate on Eileen Northcourt.

Blue Lakes Inns
Corporate Headquarters
2435 DeQuarella Dr.
Midland, Michigan 48640
1-(800) BLUE INN

Dear Mr. & Mrs. Eder:

This is a letter of introduction for Eileen Northcourt who will be managing your property during your two-week vacation period, scheduled for July 14 through July 28. Ms. Northcourt is scheduled to arrive at your property on July 13th, and has been told that she will be oriented to your property upon her arrival. Her schedule has been planned to allow her to remain on your property through July 29, which should permit ample opportunity for transition. Her schedule has her spending two weeks at each property and then allows 5 days off to travel to the next property.

Eileen Northcourt is a college student from Johnson & Wales University majoring in Hospitality Management. She is in her junior year, and has worked in restaurants for the past five summers. Her grades are strong and she has completed her finance courses, computer courses, and marketing class. Her recommendations were exceptionally strong and noted her talents for working with people. Additionally, Eileen is fluent in Spanish.

Have a wonderful time on your vacation! If you have any questions about these arrangements, please contact me at the Corporate Offices, ext. 385.

Sincerely Yours,

Sydney Bantam
Relief Manager Coordinator

Eileen Northcourt's Arrival

Eileen pulled into the parking lot around 9:00 a.m. She parked her red Saturn at the back of the parking lot and walked to the front desk, carefully evaluating the exterior of the property. The property looked clean and well maintained. As the parking lot was nearly full, Eileen assumed that the Inn had good occupancy the night before, and made a mental note to check the rooms forecast for the number of stay-overs. She felt it important to communicate directly with any stay overs to determine their needs and to let them know that she was managing the property while the Eders were on vacation.

Rose was working the front desk when Eileen entered and introduced herself. Rose welcomed her warmly, asked how her trip was, and then notified Pete that Eileen had arrived. One of the guest rooms had been taken out of inventory for Eileen's stay. Rose handed her the key and suggested that they all meet back at the desk at 11:00 a.m. The three of them would go to Beningo's for lunch. Eileen agreed, thanked Rose for the key, and then went to her room to settle in.

Eileen, Peter, and Rose drove to the restaurant in Eileen's car so she could get used to the area. Rose brought along a list of the competitors, the schedule for the next three weeks, and the rooms' forecast for the month. Peter explained how the reservation computer system worked. Peter also explained that the time frame for delivering forecasts to corporate must be punctual. In the past ten years they have never been late and their forecasted numbers and their actual numbers have been close. On several occasions, they had received letters of recognition from Hughes and Zellers. Peter went on to explain they always exceeded the expectations of corporate in both operational standards and revenue generated. Rose added that they were not in the habit of

Food and Beverage Within Lodging Operations

"troubling" the corporate office with lots of questions. Rose and Peter actually preferred to correspond via written communication so that there was little room for error. This was especially true for communications regarding operational standards. The corporate office took care of all marketing, and the Eders faxed in reports on the competitor's activities/rates every three to five days.

Eileen had a feeling that this operation was going to be easy to manage because so many of the corporate standards were not only met, but exceeded. The overall organization was easy to follow, and many procedures had come from well-thought-out systems of operation. Furthermore, the people were really hospitable and friendly here.

The Eders Depart

Rose and Peter were all packed and on their way to leave, but as had been their tradition, they checked on the night audit and room assignments before leaving. Eileen came down to meet with the night auditor and discovered they had already approved all the assignments for the day. She was accustomed to owners doing "one last thing" before leaving, and took no offense.

Eileen sat down at the office computer to log onto the corporate Internet e-mail account—only to discover that the software for the modem was not installed. It seems that just the fax software was in place for sending reports to the corporate office. She installed the modem software and then called corporate for the assigned account number needed to establish an Internet account for this sight. Over the next few days, as time allowed, Eileen set up a World Wide Web (WWW) site to take advantage of the Texas market. It was really a compliment to the Eders that they had such up-to-date hardware and software. It appeared that each time corporate had recommended a computer update, they had done it. Eileen was able to take the "older "units and piece together another station which had everything except the fax. Eileen also spent some time with Jim Rodrigues showing him how to set up spread sheets which could generate more charts and graphs to support the numbers forecasted. In week two, Eileen started to include these in her reports to corporate. Jim's reaction was very favorable—he even brought in his own color printer to the office for the second system. Eileen stayed in touch with the corporate office through e-mail. Eileen had commented on what a stellar operation the Eders had here, and that someday she herself would like to own such a successful property. The operation has not yet realized any new customers from the WWW site, but it usually takes four to six weeks to track these leads, according to corporate. It has been interesting for Eileen to track the improvement to reservations that some of the other properties have realized. Corporate put Eileen through 10 seminar hours to learn how to develop WWW site pages and track results. It was easy for her to track the results of other properties through the Internet.

The Eders Return

Rose and Peter Eder returned right on schedule about 3 p.m. the last day of their vacation. They trusted Eileen, corporate had always sent very capable people to run their operation. It was interesting to them that this was the first time corporate had sent a female manager. They were well rested and had enjoyed their travels, but were also quite happy to be home.

The Eders stopped at the front desk before unloading. They wanted to check the rooms forecast for the week and to be sure that Eileen had sent the required monthly reports to corporate. Pete and Rose were very pleased to find Eileen working at the desk and observed that everything seem to be well organized. Eileen welcomed the Eders back and asked about their trip. When they inquired about property operations, Eileen handed them a folder and explained that she had compiled the corporate monthly reports, rooms forecasts and desk log digests for them to review. Before Pete could ask Eileen about the timeliness of report submissions, Eileen produced a fax log sheet that verified the time and date that the communications were made. Pete was pleased with Eileen's efficiency. Rose suggested that they all go to dinner together, but Eileen declined, explaining that Jim had the night off and she would be covering for him. She encouraged the Eders to relax, unpack, and to enjoy one last day of vacation. They agreed, and told Eileen that they would meet with her in the morning.

Rose and Pete returned to their normal routine the next morning and arrived at the front desk at 5:00 a.m. Eileen was just finishing up room assignment when they arrived. They were particularly anxious to discuss the reports Eileen had generated, as they were somewhat different than reports that the Eders had traditionally submitted. In addition to the final monthly figures and comparison with figures from the proceeding year, Eileen had added a percentage column, several color graphs and charts, and a separate section comparing the Eder's operation to other BlueLake properties sharing similar characteristics. In short, while the Eders were impressed with the quality and clarity of the report, they were somewhat overwhelmed.

Eileen answered the Eder's questions with as little "techno-babble" as possible; however, they both felt a bit frustrated. Rose had felt very comfortable with the computer system and the functions they used it for prior to departing on their trip. However, she now felt intimidated by the expanded applications that Eileen had introduced. When Eileen went to check out a guest, Pete tried to reassure Rose that it would be "okay." After all, corporate had always commended them on the way things were done at their property. Just because a college student came in and jazzed things up, it didn't really mean that they needed to change anything. They would change only when corporate formally communicated the need to change. Eileen overheard the end of the conversation, and assured the Eders that she would bring them up to date on the technology before she left.

Eileen spent the next day demonstrating for the Eders the various upgrades she had made to the system. Rose and Pete were profoundly overwhelmed, but were comforted somewhat by the "cheat sheet" of functions that Eileen had compiled. She also assured them that they could call Marie Tremblay with any problems or concerns that they had. Before leaving the property, Eileen stopped at the desk to thank the Eders for the opportunity to work at their property. She complemented them on how well run their property was, and wished them success in the future.

A Word from Corporate

Two weeks later, Rose and Pete received a fax from the corporate offices complementing them on the professional appearance of the monthly reports and high monthly profits. It was strongly recommended that all future reports be submitted in a similar format. This was a challenge that the Eders were not looking forward to, but one with which they would comply. Pete decided to contact Marie Tremblay by fax regarding the request and to obtain further technical assistance. After two days, the Eders had still not received any communication from Marie

Tremblay. Pete was very disturbed by this and finally decided to call corporate directly. When he reached Marie, she informed him that she had responded to his fax via e-mail two days ago. Marie went on to ask if there was anything wrong with their computer system since they had over 267 pieces of unopened mail. Pete and Rose got out the "cheat sheet" that Eileen had left for them. They logged on to the system and began to read their mail.

Income Statement -- BlueLakes, Wichita Falls

	Jul-95	Jul-95%	Jul-94	Jul-94%	Corporate June-95	Corp. June-95
Revenue						
Rooms	$103,314.34	97.60%	$98,287.10	97.60%	$88,134.75	97.60%
PBX (Phone)	$2,540.52	2.40%	$2,416.90	2.40%	$2,167.25	2.40%
Total Sales	$105,854.86	100.00%	$100,704.00	100.00%	$90,302.00	100.00%
Cost of Sales						
Room Supplies	$15,497.15	15.00%	$14,743.07	15.00%	$8,813.48	10.00%
Royalties	$5,292.74	5.00%	$5,035.20	5.00%	$4,515.10	5.00%
Total Cost of Sales	$20,789.89	19.64%	$19,778.27	19.64%	$13,328.58	14.76%
Gross Profit	$85,064.97	80.36%	$80,925.73	80.36%	$76,973.42	85.24%
Controllable Expenses						
Payroll	$22,229.52	21.00%	$21,147.84	21.00%	$19,866.44	22.00%
Employee Benefits	$6,351.29	6.00%	$6,042.24	6.00%	$5,418.12	6.00%
Dir. Operating Exp.	$6,351.29	6.00%	$6,042.24	6.00%	$5,418.12	6.00%
Music and Entertainment	$211.71	0.20%	$201.41	0.20%	$180.60	0.20%
Advertising and Promo	$1,587.82	1.50%	$1,510.56	1.50%	$1,354.53	1.50%
Utilities	$3,175.65	3.00%	$3,021.12	3.00%	$2,709.06	3.00%
Administration & Gene.	$5,292.74	5.00%	$5,035.20	5.00%	$3,160.57	3.50%
Repair & Maintenance	$2,117.10	2.00%	$2,014.08	2.00%	$1,806.04	2.00%
Total Control Exp	$47,317.12	44.70%	$45,014.69	44.70%	$39,913.48	44.20%
Income Before Occ Costs	$37,747.84	35.66%	$35,911.05	35.66%	$37,059.94	41.04%
Occupation Costs						
Mortgage	$6,540.00	6.18%	$6,540.00	6.49%	$6,540.00	7.24%
Property Taxes	$2,750.00	2.60%	$2,750.00	2.73%	$2,750.00	3.05%
Other Taxes	$4,500.00	4.25%	$4,500.00	4.47%	$4,500.00	4.98%
Property Insurance	$6,000.00	5.67%	$6,000.00	5.96%	$6,000.00	6.64%
Interest	$500.00	0.47%	$500.00	0.50%	$500.00	0.55%
Depreciation	$10,000.00	9.45%	$10,000.00	9.93%	$10,000.00	11.07%
Total Occup. Costs	$30,290.00	218.61%	$30,290.00	30.08%	$30,290.00	33.54%
Profit Before Taxes	$7,457.84	7.05%	$5,621.05	5.58%	$6,769.94	7.50%

8

WHITE ELM ROOM

Senesac Hotel: Food and Beverage Department

Mike Toohill completed his normal morning routine, as he drove to the Senesac hotel on Friday morning. He picked up a bagel and a cup of coffee at Joe's Deli and then drove to the corner of Smith and Vine to buy a paper. This was the same routine he followed each of his six days of work each week. He knew today would be a tough one. It always was difficult coming back to work after a day off. There were so many daily business issues to deal with, and the longer term issues were always there. Sometimes he asked himself why he even bothered to try taking days off, it always seems that there was twice as much work when he returned as when he left.

As he pulled into the parking lot, he made a metal note to call Paul Shermis, the executive housekeeper, about the trash he saw. It was evident that someone had a great time last night, as evidenced by the beer bottle he saw in the planters and the toilet paper that had been thrown into the trees. Its funny, he thought, how much the dark covers up, and how much the

■ 97 ■

dawn reveals. Mike entered the hotel and stopped at the front desk. He picked up his mail and had Paul paged. He then went to his office, open his coffee and began to sort through his mail. It was 5:00 a.m.

The first item that Mike read was the Hotel Operations Log and the Kitchen Operations reports from the previous day. He had closed the operations on Wednesday evening, so he needed only to concentrate on reports from Thursday. The following items particularly caught Mike's attention:

Senesac Hotel Operations Log

Date/ Time	Information/ Entry
9/19 10:30 p.m.	Don't allow waitress Sue Martin on the property until she meets with Mike Toohill. Around 9:30p.m., Sue placed an order of pasta, shrimp and broccoli. She forgot to specify "no shrimp" per the customer's request. When she refused the order, chef Fred Sabo began to pick the shrimp out of the dish by hand. Sue refused the dish again and an argument began. Fred and Sue only stopped yelling when she threw the plate at him. The plate hit the reach-in behind the line and shattered. Sue was immediately suspended. Chris Rutledge, MOD

Senesac Hotel

Kitchen Operations Shift Report

Date: *September 19*

Shift Hours: *3 - 11 p.m.*

Weather: *Warm/ Cloudy*

Number of Reservations: *45*

Number of Covers: *81*

Number of Room Service Orders: *12*

Special(s):

Bratwurst and Warm Potato Salad $11.95

Veal w/ Plums $14.95

Returns, include reason:

one—Room Service burger (rm. 224) -- guest said was cold.

Waste, include reason: *None*

Submitted by: *Fred Sabo, Chef*

Received by MOD

Chris Rutlege

Time Stamp: **19Sept94 - 23:24**

Mike picked up the phone and dialed Johnson Kim's and Hans Zimmer's extensions. Neither manager was in, so Mike left voice mail messages for them to call him as soon as they arrived. He made an additional note to call Georgia on this matter as well. It was becoming very clear that the MOD method of managing the restaurant was ineffective. This was the third time in the last two months that kitchen and dining room staff in the White Elm had been in a dispute. Mike had been lobbying the EOC to approve the hiring of an Assistant Restaurant Manager to provide better support and supervision for the White Elm staff in the restaurant manager's (Johnson Kim) absence.

Mike had finished his first cup of coffee and left the office to get a second cup. The White Elm dining room staff had just arrived and were starting to brew the first pot of the day. He informed them that the hotel had sold out the night before and kidded them about bracing themselves for the rush. As he waited for the coffee to finish brewing, he looked out of the restaurant window and could see the housemen picking up the mess in the parking lot.

Coffee in hand, Mike returned to his office and picked up the paper, read his horoscope and Ann Landers, and then turned back to the front page. The following article caught his eye:

Hastings man arrested in serious accident

DENNISON, PA - A Pennsylvania man faces charges of driving under the influence, reckless endangerment and leaving the scene of an accident, after a collision on Route 93 in which a man, and two women, were seriously injured last night according to police.

The victims of the accident, who have not been identified, pending notification of relatives, were airlifted from the scene of the accident to Emerson County Hospital.

Witnesses with cell phones called police to report the license plate of a car driving erratically on route 93 moments before the crash occurred. At about 8:15 p.m. the car carrying the injured travelers was hit from behind causing it to flip onto the median strip. The two passengers who were not wearing seat belts were thrown from the car. The driver of the car causing the accident did not stop at the scene.

Mario DeGregario, 28, of Hastings, was stopped by police on Route 93 at approximately 8:25 p.m. DeGregorio was arrested on charges including driving to endanger serious injury resulting, driving under the influence, speeding and leaving the scene of an accident. DeGregario was held last night on $2,000 cash bail and was scheduled for an arraignment today in Dennison District Court.

Upon reading the article, Mike called the front desk to see if Hans Zimmer had arrived yet. He could feel his stress level rising. Once again, there was another "fire" to put out in the kitchen. Mario had been a good worker, but Mike had questioned his maturity level. Hans, however, was perhaps Mario's greatest advocate and had personally invested himself in Mario's development. A quick glance at the schedule revealed that that although Mario had been off the day before (thankfully), he was scheduled in at 8:00 a.m. Concerned with the White Elm facing a busy morning with the hotel sold out, Mike was anxious to fill Hans in on the recent events.

The relationship between Hans and Mike had become increasingly strained over the last several months. They had once been a successful working team, sharing a joint vision for the White Elm room and the food and beverage department, until, 2 months ago, the food and beverage department had placed the focus on banquet and catering functions. The White Elm's niche as a breakfast and sometimes lunch and dinner spot had been accepted by the hotel and corporation management. However, within the last 60 days, a sharp decrease from the low 70%s to the low

50%s in hotel occupancy (300 rooms/ rack rate between $125.00 and $150) has pressured the Food and beverage department to generate more revenue at higher percentage of profit.

As a result, last Wednesday, Eric Wickford came to Mike and asked him to prepare a proposal to reposition the White Elm Room from its present "Liberty Bell Theme" to a more popular concept. This important project needed to be completed by the following Monday. Always pleased with a challenge, Mike set to work on the proposal which advocated a more contemporary, health conscious menu focus that would appeal to business people in the surrounding community in addition to guests in the hotel. On Monday morning Mike brought his finished, thoroughly researched proposal, to Mr. Wickford. He was surprised to find Hans Zimmer meeting with Mr. Wickford when he arrived. Eric invited him into the office, accepted his proposal, and then asked him to sit down.

"Well, this is great, I have two committed Managers," Eric commented. It seemed that Hans had developed a competing plan for the White Elm and had submitted his own, unsolicited proposal. Prior to coming to the Senesac, Hans had owned his own restaurant and catering business "Hans' Treats" which specialized in Fine German cuisine. Coincidentally, Hans' proposal was similarly focused. Eric coughed and cleared his throat, "You two are great! And lets remember that two minds are better than one! So, here's what we're going to do. Mike and Hans, you two meet, review each other's proposal . . . and come back to me on Friday with a final proposal. Work it out. Chose one or combine them or whatever. Just keep in mind the if revenues don't increase, you can kiss your bonus good-bye. Mrs. Senesac wants action."

Food and Beverage Within Lodging Operations

Now, not only did Mike have to resolve the issues with Hans regarding the White Elm proposal, but here were two more issues to resolve—the incident between Fred and Sue from the previous night, and the restaurant chef, Mario's, car accident. While he was waiting for Hans to arrive, Mike began to review his notes from their previous conversations and the independent demographic information he had complied. In his research, Mike found that 45% of the guests in the hotel were repeat guests. Mike also found that the majority of room nights were generated by the businesses surrounding the hotel and that most of these reservations were made by company representatives living and/or working within a 15 mile radius of the hotel. Sixty-two percent of restaurant guests are registered at the hotel. The remainder of guests came from the surrounding community.

Mike took one last sip of his coffee, crushed the paper cup, and tossed it into the wastebasket, scoring a "three pointer." Hans Zimmer appeared in the doorway, and gave Mike a round of applause. "Come on in Hans. We have a lot to discus," Mike said as he rose from his chair.

Background

The present day setting is in a medium-sized hotel in the metropolitan area of Hastings, Pennsylvania, with interstate exit access of less than half a mile. Hastings is a suburb of Philadelphia and approximately 8 miles from the Philadelphia Airports. Leona Senesac is the absentee owner of the Hotel. She presently lives in the midwest to be close to her grandchildren.

The Senesac Hotel was built in 1983, has a large glass atrium and is four stories tall. A detached parking garage is adjacent to the hotel and is free to patrons staying more than two nights. The White Elm Room, the lobby restaurant, does a heavy breakfast business and has seating for 80 people. A lunch and dinner menu is also offered. The restaurant primarily serves hotel guests. The room service menu is limited and not off of the White Elm Room menu. Hours of the restaurant are 6:00 a.m. to 9:30 a.m. for breakfast, 11:00 a.m. to 2:00 p.m. for Lunch and 5:00 p.m. to 11:00 p.m. for dinner. Room service hours are 6:30 a.m. until 11:00 p.m. Three function rooms and two conference rooms are also available throughout the Sales and Catering Office. Sales and Catering is open Monday through Friday from 9:00 a.m. to 6:00 p.m. and on Saturday's from 9:00 a.m. to 1:00 p.m. The White Elm averages 2 turns at breakfast, 1.5 turns for lunch and .85 turns for dinner, except for dinner on the weekend when it is 1-1.25 turns. The breakfast menu runs between $3.95-$6.95; lunch runs between $6.50-$8.90; dinners $10.95-$14.95.

Management

An executive operating committee (EOC) oversees key decisions in the hotel. The committee is comprised of the management team—Eric Wickford: General Manager; Lucy Hall: Resident Manager; Mike Toohill: Food and Beverage Manager; Georgia Mayfield: Director of Human Resources; Chris Rutledge: Rooms Division Manager, and Melvin Wagner: Director of Sales and Catering.

Within the Food and Beverage Department, Mike Toohill relies on a key management staff—Monica Harris: Assistant Food and Beverage Manager; Hans Zimmer: Executive Chef; Mario DeGregario: Restaurant Chef; Ravn Sabol: Banquet Chef, and Johnson Kim: Restaurant Manager.

Management Team Profiles

Eric Wickford has been the manager for five years which is also the length of the current owner's tenure. Prior to that he had management experience in the Boston area. Eric is 57 years old and after his last physical, required by the company, was told to "get more exercise." He has a B.S. degree in business from Penn State and has been married to Martha, a domestic engineer for 35 years. Eric and Martha have six children, two of who are now employed in the hospitality field. In the interest of increasing hotel occupancy and food and beverage revenues, Mr. Wickford has been personally negotiating with several airlines to use the hotel for both crew and "distressed traveler: accommodations."

Mike Toohill has been with the company for almost five years and has a degree in business from Penn State. Mike is divorced, 55 years old and is known as a hard worker. Mr. Toohill has been working on a plan to present to the EOC so that the lobby restaurant can be repositioned in the market. The White Elm Room menu currently reflects what is best described as a "Liberty Bell" Theme and offers traditional American fare. Mike wishes to capitalize on the presence of local businesses by offering light, quick-service meals, and by incorporating more contemporary favorites such as Grilled Chicken Caesar Salad.

Monica Harris joined the Senesac Hotel immediately after graduation and has been with the Hotel for 3 years. She earned as A.S. degree in Culinary Arts from C.I.A. and a B.S. degree in Hotel, Restaurant, Institutional Management from University of Wisconsin at Stout. Monica is very well respected at the Hotel and within the Senesac Hospitality Company. She has consistently earned above, average performance reviews and has been identified as showing great promise in her career. Mike Toohill and Monica have an especially close working relationship.

Hans Zimmer is the Executive Chef and has been with the Senesac Hospitality Company for 3 years; he transferred in from another property 18 months ago. He is 38 years old and as a second generation immigrant he has strong ties to the local German community. Chef Zimmer has a Bachelors degree in Liberal Arts from the University of Missouri and a A.O.S. degree in Culinary Arts from a technical school located in Florida. Prior to coming to the Senesac Company, he owned and operated a catering business, "Hans' Treats," which was forced to close after 4 1/2 years of operation. Hans has been married for 10 years and has two daughters who are active in ballet. There has been some conflict between Chef Zimmer and Mr. Toohill, as Hans has put forth his own ideas on repositioning the White Elm Room. He feels that the Hotel's restaurant should become an exclusive "showcase" specializing in fine German Cuisine.

Johnson Kim is a US citizen, but he is also a fairly recent immigrant. A member of a tight knit Asian family, he lives with his brother's family. His brother holds a key leadership position with one of the local software companies. Johnson has a Master's Degree in Computer Science that he earned in his native country. However, this true career interest lies in the Hospitality Industry, in part due to the experience he gained working in the family restaurant before he came to the United States. Mr. Kim has been with the hotel for 2 years. During that time, there has been an increase in staff turnover as well as a decrease in staff overtime. There is no Assistant Restaurant Manager, so in Johnson's absence, the White Elm Room is the responsibility of the manager on duty (MOD).

Marketing Position

The Senesac Hotel is located in a stanch German ethnic community. The area surrounding the hotel is fast becoming an international business center for light manufacturing and computer technology support. As a result, the hotel is primarily targeted at the business traveler with some seasonal business centered around the leisure traveler. Function business is from local industries who need training and meeting facilities. The room mix includes both suites and traditional hotel rooms.

Hotel occupancy has been 58%. Food and Beverage operations have long been considered a primary revenue source for the hotel's balance sheet. Local businesses have some interest in off premise catering. The hotel has a swimming pool and shuttle service within a ten mile radius.

Additional Information

The waitstaff during breakfast and lunch shifts of the White Elm Room is made up of older, long-term employees (8 years of more). Young, college-age workers staff the restaurant during the evening hours. The restaurant has established policies that include "on-call" scheduling for all employees 2 days per month, tip pooling, and self-bussing of tables. The front of the house has no responsibility for room service operations.

The restaurant kitchen was recently remodeled and includes separate order pick-up areas for dining room and room service. The dish/pot washing staff is non-English-speaking and diverse ethnically. In addition to preparing meals for room service and the White Elm Room, the kitchen is also responsible for any special request meals for the banquet department (dietetic, vegetarian, etc.).

9

OUTBREAK AT THE GATES HOTEL

Food Poisoning Outbreak at Gates Hotel — 78 Hospitalized

BAKER, CA — Local hospitals were overwhelmed yesterday by a flood of people complaining of nausea, vomiting, severe cramping, and diarrhea. Over 170 people were examined in area emergency rooms, while the majority were treated and released. This morning 78 people remain hospitalized.

All of the people who became ill were members of the cancer survival support group, Second Life, staying at the Gates Hotel for a conference. The conference's first event yesterday was a buffet brunch. Within 6 hours, several people had become ill and were transported to Center City Hospital. As the day progressed and the number of people feeling ill increased, local officials activated the local emergency disaster plans to avoid any one of the local hospitals becoming flooded with patients. Everett, Turners, St. Mary's, and Mitchell Hospitals were all involved in treating patients from Gates.

At a press conference late last evening, officials from all of the hospitals involved stated that the exact cause of the outbreak had not yet been identified, but that Salmonella bacteria was strongly suspected as the culprit. Dr. Daniel Galipeau stated that treating the patients had been especially difficult as many were actively being treated for cancer and had weakened immune systems as a result. "We do not typically experience such severe symptoms associated with food-borne illness. The victims of this outbreak are especially vulnerable. Currently, of the 78 people hospitalized 10 are in intensive care. The remainder are classified as being in serious or fair condition. They are being treated with antibiotics and intravenous fluids. Oncologists have been called in, as have counselors to support the families.

The Health Department ordered the kitchen of the Gates Hotel closed and has taken samples of food for testing. Results of the cultures will be announced within 48 hours. Officials from the Gates Hotel could not be reached for comment.

Late last night it was learned that the hotel had moved all of its guests to other hotel properties in the area.

Gates Hotel
Banquet Event Order

Post As: Second Life Sunday Brunch
Event Name: Brunch/ Meeting
Group: Second Life Survivors
Address: 1456 Perry Miller Blvd. **Billing**:
  Esleeck, CA 92131   Direct Bill
Phone: (619) 635-4267
FAX: (619) 635-4268 **Amount Received:**
Group Contact: Arlon T. Adams $2000.00 deposit
On-Site-Contact: same

DAY	DATE	TIME	FUNCTION	EXP	GTE
SUN	8/20/95	9:30 a.m. to 12:30 p.m.	Brunch/ Meeting	225	

All food and beverage prices are subject to an 18% service charge and a 7% state tax. Guarantee figures cancellations, and charges must be given 72 hours prior, or the number of guests will be considered the guarantee. To conform the above arrangements, this contract must be signed and returned.

Engagor Signature:

Date:

BEO # 003070

Gates Hotel
Maitre D' Function Report

Name of Function: Second Life Sunday Brunch

Contact Person: Dr. Arlon T. Adams

Function Maitre D': Jody Curpadi

The function went off on schedule. Dr. Adams arrived at 10:45 a.m. to review the set-up. Jerry O'Brian gave him instructions on the operation of the audio–visual equipment.

The guests were pleased with the quality of the food, however during the rush at 10:30 a.m. we had trouble keeping the buffet stocked. There was also a problem with several trays of eggs benedict. The guests complained that the eggs were not heated all the way through. The problem was quickly remedied by Chef Ranieri. In addition, several pitchers of Orange Juice were poured out because a number of people said that it tasted funny. We ended up replacing the fresh squeezed OJ with concentrate during the last hour of the function. Also, there was a problem with the pastry cream in the eclairs and the fruit tarts. I noticed that they were runny and asked the chef about it. He said just to keep an eye on the dessert table, and if the desserts started to "look bad," to just replace them. There were also several coffee creamers that curdled.

At 11:00 a.m., Dr. Adams began his presentation. He requested that we stop service and clearing during his 45-minute presentation. During his presentation the overhead projector bulb burned out. There was not a spare bulb in the projector; however we were able to replace the bulb and get the projector operational again within 15 minutes. Dr. Adams showed the video during this time. We apologized for the inconvenience. At 12:00 p.m., we resumed service and clearing.

Actual Guest Count: 230

Maitre D' Signature: _____

Date:_____

Outbreak Continues: Two Die as Gates Hotel Closes

BAKER, CA — At a press conference early this morning, Dr. Daniel Galipeau of St. Mary's Hospital reported that 2 people, who had been hospitalized in the ICU, have died. Their names have not been released, pending notification of relatives. To date, 83 people have been hospitalized following a buffet brunch at the Gates Hotel yesterday morning. When asked about the prognosis of those still hospitalized, Dr. Galipeau was reluctant to say anything other than that "We are currently in a wait and see position. We will continue to do everything possible."

Officials say that members of the Second Life Cancer Support Group were gathered at the Gates hotel for their annual conference. Within 6 hours of the Brunch, the first of the victims began to complain of symptoms including fever, cramping, diarrhea, and vomiting. As of this morning a total of 200 people had been examined at area emergency rooms.

Because of the large number of ill people, the area emergency catastrophe plan had to be activated. The emergency catastrophe provides support for area hospitals in terms of volunteer support as well as procedures such as care rationing and triage. As a result of the outbreak, elective procedures were canceled.

Health officials expect to confirm later today the source of the outbreak. Dr. Emily Lister stated ". . . that salmonella bacteria suspected, however until test are in, we can not firmly identify the cause of this outbreak. In fact, more than one biological hazard may be involved.". Health officials have taken the precaution of closing the hotel and sealing the premises to determine the source of the outbreak.

Despite numerous attempts, officials of the Gates Hotel have not been reached for comment. All guests were moved to other hotel properties last evening. The Gates Hotel voluntarily closed its doors at 11:00 p.m. after the health department required the closing of the kitchen. Mrs. Addy Newell, who had been staying at the Gates and was not a member of the Second Life organization, said that the staff had been courteous in assisting her relocation to the Rose Cliff Motel. She said there was no indication as to when the Gates Hotel might reopen.

Families of those hospitalized have been provided with transportation to and from the hospital by the Gates Hotel Shuttle van. The Second Life Conference was scheduled to conclude this evening with a farewell dinner dance.

Reportedly, several families have contacted legal representation.

The phone rang and Al put down the paper, rubbed his forehead and picked up the phone. "Hello, Albert Hinckle speaking." "Al, its Dana. Have you see today's paper?" Al could always count on Dana Compton, the resident manager of the Gates Hotel, to keep him up to date on things. She had been invaluable to him in recent months. In fact, during his first weeks as General manager, six months ago, he let her "run the property" while he got accustomed to things. She was committed to the hotel and management team.

Al continued: "Yes, I have. Two deaths. This looks really bad for Gates. I can't believe the health department has quarantined the property! This could be enough to put us under, what with no rooms revenue, no function revenue, paying for guest to stay at other hotels. . . and if we can't reopen by the Thursday, we'll have an even bigger problem. The hotels that took our guests."

"Let me guess," interrupted Dana, "they're sold out for the weekend."

"Yeah, and so were we, Dana" added Al. "We are losing a full week of 100% occupancy. The Second Life group's room block was negotiated at a rate of $75.00/night double occupancy. We are now PAYING them to stay elsewhere at a higher rate! . . .

Food and Beverage Within Lodging Operations

and then there is the whole issue of what we are losing in F&B revenues . . ."

"All that aside, Al, don't you think its time that the Gates Hotel issued a statement? I mean we look really bad right now. The hotel is closed and the press hasn't heard a word from any Gates official. Channel 12 has been broadcasting hourly updates on the "Gates Plague" from in front of the hotel—complete with a score card of how many ill, hospitalized, and dead." Dana ended the sentence with a forceful slap on a table that Al could hear through the phone.

"Dana, I have spoken with legal counsel, and until an exact source for the outbreak can be determined, we have been advised against issuing a statement. Making a public statement about the problem might be construed as taking responsibility for the problem in a court of law. Once the exact cause of the outbreak has been identified, a preliminary statement will be issued. Beyond that, there isn't much to do except sit and wait. I have been in contact with Gates Hotel owners and they have asked me to strictly follow the recommendations of counsel." Al sighed. "I know that this is frustrating, Dana."

"What about the staff? They are asking if we are going to reopen. The kitchen staff feels guilty, and this is really hurting our team. Not knowing anything, other than what is in the press, and having management remain silent is making the staff really uncomfortable. I really think we need to be more proactive."

"Yes, Dana, you do have a point. I agree that the staff needs to be reassured. But I am afraid with so much still unknown, that we will generate more uncertainty than we will alleviate. And if someone leaks to the press, we could have even bigger problems. I'll call you once we know more and thank you for your concern. You are always so dedicated. I'll talk to you soon. Good bye, Dana."

"OK (sigh), I'll wait to hear more." Dana hung up the phone and then threw a book across the room in frustration.

The Gates Hotel Crisis—Where do we go from here?

BAKER, CA — Since Sunday, a total of 215 people have been treated at local hospitals for symptoms stemming from exposure to contaminated food at a brunch at the Gates Hotel. Two people have died as a result of exposure and several others remain hospitalized. Cultures analyzed by the health department have revealed that two types of bacteria have been identified — salmonella and staphylococcus —as the cause of the illness. According to Dr. Emily Lister of the Baker County Health Department, evidence of contamination has been found in the eggs and dairy products used to prepare many of the dishes served.

The Gates Hotel has remained closed since the first day of the outbreak. Following a complete inspection of the property, it is anticipated that the hotel will reopen next week. To date. there has been no official word from the Gates Hotel.

Events like the Gates Hotel outbreak touch all of the community, whether directly or indirectly. Baker is a family community that prides itself on its beautiful scenery and local activities. Every summer, hundreds of families flock to the Baker area for vacations filled with hiking in local parks and cooling off at the Frolic Water Park. Just as the recent e. coli outbreaks have tarnished the reputations of certain restaurants, Baker is suffering the effects of the food poisoning outbreak at the Gates Hotel.

In an interview conducted last night by phone, Dr. Adams, President of Second Life, said that he and his group intend to pursue legal action against the Gates Hotel. "You enter into an agreement with a hotel to hold an event to CELEBRATE living life despite cancer, and because of their carelessness, more than 90% of the group becomes ill! This annual conference is our major fund-raising event. Each attendee paid a conference fee of $300.00, that in part was to cover the cost of meals. We carefully budgeted $81.00 per person for food and beverage events during the two-day conference. Now, many of our members are looking to Second Life to refund their conference fees. We simply cannot afford to do as they request. The Gates Hotel should take responsibility for the tragedy they have caused."

Sergio Carter, a spokesperson for the regional organization of Hospitality Professionals released a statement assuring the public that all member hotels and restaurants are working to minimize the impact of the Gates Hotel closing. "It is important to remember." said Mr. Carter in his statement, "that while things like the food poisoning outbreak at the Gates Hotel do happen, it is an isolated incident. The Gates Hotel has operated for many years without a single incident. The truth is, that while Salmonella and Staph bacteria are responsible this time, keep in mind that no member of the hotel's staff has been found at fault or for that matter found to be ill. It was probably a variety of factors that caused the problem [at the Gates Hotel]. Perhaps the reason the symptoms were so severe was because many of the attendees were cancer patients. I personally assure the public everything possible is being done to assist those inconvenienced during this crisis."

Property Information

The Gates Hotel is a budget hotel property located near Baker, California, and has rack rates ranging from $65.00 to $85.00/ night, based on double occupancy. There are a number of competing hotels in the area with room rates averaging $70.00 to $95.00 per night, double occupancy. The Gates Hotel has 250 guest rooms, 70% are standard hotel rooms, and the remaining 30% were renovated as mini suites with wetbars 5 years ago. Occupancy rate has been maintained at 87% for the past four years. The Gates Hotel's location near the Frolic Water park, a major attraction for families, has helped to maintain the current occupancy percentage.

The hotel offers 4 connecting function rooms (capacity: 80 to 120 people each) and 3 conference rooms (seating 15 people). In the lobby is located the Gateway Cafe restaurant, seating 72 guests. The Cafe is open for breakfast, lunch, and dinner, seven days a week and offers room service 6:00 a.m. to 10:00 p.m. Food and beverage operations contribute 18% of overall property revenues.

The property is independently owned and has operated since 1968. There have been three major hotel renovations over the years. A major kitchen renovation is planned for late September and early October.

## 10

The Fussy Frog Family Restaurant

The Fussy Frog Restaurant

Located on Route 18, just outside Portland, The Fussy Frog is the ideal place for a delicious meal! Bring the whole family or just someone special and dig into one of our scrumptious dinners. We have something for everyone, -- fresh fish, oversized steaks, rotisserie chicken, or the dinner special of the evening. Our prices are reasonable, so even dessert will fit into your budget. So hop on down to the Fussy Frog for a wonderful evening and a great meal right near by!

Nightly Specials

On Your Birthday, Dinner's on Us! *

Seniors Dine at 20% off from 5-6 p.m. **

The Fussy Frog Restaurant

Family owned and operated since 1957
Route 18
Winckham, Maine
Hours: 7 days a week 11:00a.m. to 11:00p.m.

* with proper ID, buy one dinner, get the birthday meal on the house.
** with proper ID, seniors 55 and over get 20% off their total food bill.

The Spencer Family

The Fussy Frog Family Restaurant has been the mainstay of the restaurant community in Portland, Maine, area since 1957. The operation is known for its home-style cooking, fresh fish, and reasonable prices. Dick and Edy Spencer founded the Fussy Frog just after their second son, Andrew, was born. In fact, the name of the restaurant was taken from the Andy's childhood nickname.

Over the years, the business grew, as did their family, and by the late 1960s all of their eight children were working in the operation before or after school, on weekends and when they were home from the college. It was understood by the whole family that the Fussy Frog was to be treated like a member of the family. It was a commitment that the Spencers took seriously.

The elder Spencers continued to oversee the operation, while their children, with the exception of Andy, went on to other careers. Andy and his wife, Becky, took over the day to day management of the Fussy Frog in 1988. However, Dick and Edy continued to spend hours each day at the restaurant chatting with their guests and making sure things were still running to perfection.

Business Over the Years at the Fussy Frog

The Fussy Frog's location on Route 18 was a wise choice. Route 18 was the main travel route through Portland until the interstate was built. However, the building of the interstate did not hurt business at the Fussy Frog, since the main on and off ramps were located less than one-half mile from the restaurant.

There were several motels located near the Fussy Frog. Directly behind the restaurant was an 80-room motel, and across the side road was another motel with 125 rooms. Both of these operations existed before the Fussy Frog was built. In the mid 1970s, two additional hotel chainsopened properties on Route 18. The Suisse Chalet, a national hotel chain, was built on property adjacent to the Fussy Frog. The Hotel Portland was a regional hotel, located 2 miles north of the Spencer's operation on the opposite side of Route 18. Hotel Portland's location was close to the interstate on and off ramps, and had signs visible from the highway. Numerous retail shops, such as K-Mart, WalMart, Sports Authority, and Lechmere, opened on Route 18 as the suburban area around the interstate began to grow.

Over the years, The Fussy Frog saw numerous businesses come and go. A drive-in movie theater was built across Route 18 in 1956, closed in 1978 and bulldozed in 1990. In 1972, a 14-theater movie cinema opened 1 mile north of the Fussy Frog on Route 18. Until 1990, the Fussy Frog was virtually the only full-service restaurant on Route 18 for a 10 mile span. Its generous curb cut and excellent signage made the Fussy Frog seem like a beacon to the hungry traveling along Route 18. Business boomed, and Dick Spencer was fond of saying he needed wheelbarrows to take it all to the bank.

In November of 1990, a new full-service restaurant opened next door to the Suisse Chalet on the side bordering the Fussy Frog. *East Side Mario's* was a full-service Italian Restaurant complete with an interior decor designed to mimic Little Italy in New York. With the opening of the new operation, the Fussy Frog saw the number of guests they served from the Suisse Chalet decrease by 50%. The Spencers tried using incentive coupons to entice guest to cross the road to the Fussy Frog, but the campaign did not generate much of a return.

In the Spring of 1993, a second full service operation opened 1/10 of a mile from the Fussy Frog. Once again, guest counts at the Spencers' operation dropped, when *Ryan's Steak House* opened on the same side of Route 18 as the both the Fussy Frog and East Side Mario's. Ryan's Steak House was a national chain, specializing in generous cuts of beef and grilled chicken dishes, served in a rustic atmosphere. They did not take reservations, and a wait of 45 minutes on a Saturday night was normal.

The Spencers chose to respond by investing in a $85,000 renovation of the property. The building was refronted and expanded to accommodate small functions of 60 guests. This, the Spencers believed, would give them an advantage over their competition. In additional to the 150 seat a la carte dining, they would be now be able to cater to meetings and receptions.

Marketing Plans

In the early years, Dick and Edy Spencer did not actively develop a concrete marketing plan. The Spencers had taken care over the years to monitor the base of their customers stream. Most of the local clientele were well know to the staff. Even if they were not known by name, they were certainly known by face, and the Spencers made a point of welcoming them warmly each time they came to the Fussy Frog.

It wasn't until fortunes began to change that the need for an intensive marketing plan became clear. The Spencers' first attempt at advertising came in placing advertisements in Church bulletins and in flyers placed at local hotel/motels. When Andy and Becky took over the operation, they developed a more sophisticated marketing plan and committed 2% of annual revenues to support the plan. They recognized the need to both develop a strong following from the year-round community as well as summer tourists. As a result, two approaches were developed.

To attract local residents, the Fussy Frog contacted a coupon mailing company. Three times a year, the Fussy Frog participated in mailings for a fee of $350.00 per mailing. This provided a three-color 8 1/2 by 4 inch coupon, mailed with an assortment of coupons from other operations to targeted zipcode areas. The coupon offered redeemers a 2-for-1 dinner deal, Monday through Friday evenings. In addition, the Fussy Frog developed a "Children Pay What They Weigh" program, on Wednesday nights. In an attempt to build sales from travelers, coupons for a 15% meal discount appeared in seasonal tourist guides and in guest service racks in area hotels/ motels.

These strategies worked very well initially. However, as competition increased these returns began to falter. New attempts to market the operation included print ads the local papers and radio ads, sponsoring the rush hour traffic reports. Despite these changes, sales at the Fussy Frog did not rebound and in fact they continued to see profits fall. Several staff were laid off as business continue to slump. Route 18 was as busy as it had always been, but the travelers were opting for well-known names. While, the Fussy Frog was well known locally, it simply did not have the draw of their national competition.

Moving to the Hotel Portland

Hotel Portland had been very successful as a rooms property over the years. Known for its nice but moderately priced accommodations, the chain had done well and was continuing to perform against the better known national chains. This reputation had helped grow the once single location to a franchise of six properties throughout Maine.

It was well know that the food and beverage services at the Hotel Portland were notoriously poor, so much so, in fact, that many a radio talk show host poked fun at the operations. The hotel provided a full-service restaurant, a lounge, and a banquet facility for 125 guests. The restaurant rarely served anyone but the hotel guests, the lounge had become a hangout for those with questionable characters, and the last banquet function was held six months ago.

The Hotel Portland was seriously considering closing the food and beverage operation, when Andrew and Rebecca Spencer came to the owners with a proposal to take over the food and beverage operations, at a fixed annual lease of $36,000 per year for 5 years. After the first 2 years, the Portland Hotel would receive percentage of sales in addition to the annual rent. This percentage was set at 1% to 3%.

In return, the Fussy Frog would close, sell its present Route 18 location and move to the Hotel Portland. All equipment from the current location would be moved to the new location. This transition would require a 2-month closing of the food and beverage operations at the Hotel Portland and the closing of the Fussy Frog. It would be the first time that the Fussy Frog had been closed for more than one week in the operation's 40-year history. Furthermore, the after first year, the Spencers would have the option of opening additional

Fussy Frog operations in any or all remaining Hotel Portland locations.

On August 16, 1996, the Fussy Frog closed its doors with a bon voyage party. Banner signs were placed on the roof, and over the main signs announcing that the Fussy Frog was taking a trip north on Route 18, and that he'd be seeing you all in a couple of months.

The Fussy Frog is Now Located at the Hotel Portland.

The move to the Hotel Portland resulted in several changes. The new facility provided the Fussy Frog with an opportunity to change its current image as a place to bring the family to a place to enjoy an evening out. They attempted to build this new image by developing a campaign to build business in the Bar/Lounge by offering free appetizers on Friday and Saturday nights, and pizza on weekend afternoons during football season. The new facility was comprised of 102 seats in the dining room and 37 seats in the bar. The Spencers were able to hire back some of the staff they had laid off in the previous year and still maintain labor costs at 22%. This percentage was anticipated to drop during the summer months when family members came to Maine for the summer season.

However, the bulk of the Fussy Frog's guests continued to be families and travelers. Analysis of sales revealed that the 67% of guests were families, 12% of guests were seniors, and the remainder were a mix of singles and couples. The guest check average for the Fussy Frog was $11.50; entrees ranged in price from $7 to $10 wiith desserts from $2.50 to $3.50. Dessert sales were consistently higher than beverage sales. Beverage sales made up 12% of total sales. Friday was the busiest night of the week. Saturdays and Sundays were also significant business days. Weekend table turns averaged 3.5 to 3.9.

The guest count for Saturday was almost always stronger than Sunday, with the exception of promotional weekends. The Spencers attempted to draw guests to the restaurant and bar on Sunday afternoons with a sports bar theme, complete with a buffet and several large screen televisions. Quarter-page ads were taken out in the local paper at a cost of $500 per run. The adds did generate business for the $9.95 Sports Buffet. The adds ran periodically, as they could be afforded. Andy had designated 10% of the advertising budget for print ads.

Further expansion of services considered by the Spencers consisted of a carry-out business. Their desserts had always been popular, and they felt that a display case and a bakery style carry-out area would increase sales. In addition, they were considering offering quarts of soup and baked beans for take-out sales.

The move to the new location did cause a fall off from some local clientele. This in part stemmed from the fact that in order to get to the new location, guests would be required to double back along busy Route 18. Traffic on the road made this a difficult endeavor.

Yet sales on Christmas Eve were strong. In a report submitted to the Hotel General Manger, the Spencers reported that 40% of the sales were Gift Certificate based, and singles made up 65% of the guest count. This was the busiest Christmas Eve the Fussy Frog had experienced in its history.

Business volume over the first year at the new location mimicked the Route 18 location. The months of January through March were moderate, April was very busy, and May saw the business volume drop. However, the arrival of summer tourists increased business through the summer months. September continued to be busy, as did October. The last months of the year saw a slowing of business during the weekdays, while weekends remained busy.

RISING HOPE CENTER

Stickney, MA

Author's Note: The author believes that it is important for Hospitality students to have an understanding of non-profit organizations which integrate both traditional and nontraditional aspects of the industry. This case will integrate elements of a small food service operation with child/eldercare and recreation/leisure facilities.

Introduction

The Rising Hope Center opened in 1967 as a child daycare center to serve the needs of low- to moderate- income families of Stickney, Massachusetts. A group of moderate- to high- income women founded the center as a social action project of their Temple. They were successful in rallying a team of community leaders to support and contribute to the realization of the project.

The city rendered its support by providing a facility for the center, in the form of a disused elementary school. The group, which had grown to include a cross representation of the community, incorporated and signed a 30-year agreement with the city to lease the building for one dollar a year. The newly formed corporation would be responsible for maintenance, upkeep, and insurance requirements. Day-to-day operation of the center was placed in the hands of a Center Director who reported to the Board of Directors, a group of 14 people, generally the original founders of the center.

The Rising Hope Center operated as a non-profit social service agency whose primary mission was to provide support to young families. Rising Hope qualified for and has received United Way funding since its inception. In the early years (late 1960s to early 1970s), common thinking dictated that the best way to help stabilize "at risk" families was to provide classes in parenting skills. It was assumed that low-income parents lacked sufficient skills to manage their children without guidance. Over the years, this focus has changed and the center now views its role as a secondary force influencing the family.

The Community

Stickney is an urban community located outside of Boston on the Southshore, with a population of approximately 600,000. Harvard University is within a 20-minute expressway drive from the city limits. Because of the proximity of Harvard and the greater Boston area, Stickney is noted as being an especially diverse community, as evidenced by the ethnic, religious, and financial make-up of the city. While these diverse populations interact well within the public arenas, such as the schools, distinct residential areas have developed that are not well integrated. There are well entrenched sub-communities extending several city blocks, in which the majority of residents are Afro-American, Jewish, Portuguese, Spanish, Italian, etc. Within each of these sub-communities, there exists a distinct stratification of financial resources. As a result, affluent, moderate- and low-income level families reside in close proximity, in many cases being separated only by a few city blocks. Individuals employed in the immediate area work for financial institutions or light manufacturing companies. Many are still employed in the local mills.

Social Changes

The evolution of the Rising Hope Center has been driven by shifts in both the national and local communities. The two primary forces directing change are the increasing number of two-income families, and the development of the "Sandwich Generation."

Throughout the 1970s and 1980s, the number of women entering the workforce increased substantially, and by 1980 it was estimated that women represented 43% of the workforce. This number has continued to grow, and it is estimated that by the year 2000, the number will rise to 47%. This means that 61% of women will be employed outside of the home. No longer did the term "working mother" apply only to single, low-income mothers, but women from "financially comfortable" families were also entering the workplace. This resulted in an increased number of families from all income levels requiring child daycare services. Childcare has evolved over the years from simple baby-sitting into a curriculum-based, all-day care for children, focused on developing skills. The role of caregiver is becoming more important as the number of family contact hours declines.

The term "Sandwich Generation" is an outgrowth of the graying of America. It refers to the challenges, experienced by many members of the "baby boom" generation of raising children, while also providing care for elderly parents. While childcare is often easy to secure, meaningful adult care programs are difficult to find. The successful programs that exist provide care for their clients in a dignified manner, allowing the seniors to contribute through activities and projects, in an environment that provides supervision and/or support.

Rising Hope had consistent management throughout its first two decades. The first two directors gave the Center nearly 20 years of service. In the last six years, the Center has undergone a number of management changes. The last three directors have had a combined tenure of 4 years. The current director, Mary Elliott, is completing her first year of service.

The center director is empowered by the board of directors to act on day-to-day operations, with "big" decisions requiring board approval. Each of the two long-term directors completed strategic plans for the organization and brought them to the board for approval. A strategic plan has not been developed since the departure of the second long-term director, over six years ago. Although succeeding directors have appreciated the need to plan for the future, they have not found the time to complete a new strategic plan due to the challenges of daily operations. As a result, the Board has been placed in the unfamiliar and uncomfortable role of developing the long-term plans for the center.

Most of the current board members have served since the incorporation of the center. The only board member turnover has been through parents who have 2-year tenures. Many of the directors use their board membership as a social outlet for community service, and as an opportunity to work with their friends. The majority of board members do not have business experience, and 40% do not work outside the home. The Board has a great sense of tradition and generally feels that things should be done the way they have always been done in the past, and any direct conflict should be avoided.

Another major issue impacting the center occurred during the Reagan era. The multitude of federal cuts to dependent care and job retraining programs resulted in many families losing childcare subsidies. The loss of funding left many of the Center's families unable to pay tuition at the full rate. In an effort to assist these families during the crisis, and to stem the loss of students, the Center implemented a sliding fee scale to help meet the families, abilities to pay. This was implemented with the idea that they would temporarily reduce rates while parents were in training or education programs. When the parents completed their programs and were earning higher wages, they would then return to paying the Center full tuition.

Physical Plant

The two-story building is brick, with large windows, 20-foot ceilings, hard wood floors, a centrally located kitchen, and some patches of grass around the building. During the past 27 years, new washrooms and kitchen equipment have been installed inside the building. There is no devoted parking for family and/ or employees. An access ramp for the front door was attached in 1992, in response to the ADA regulations and OSHA requirements. Each age group has an assigned room, and a maximum number of students can be enrolled, based upon licensing and teacher certification.

Present Day

Rising Hope is currently in financial trouble. Last summer's enrollment was less than 50% of capacity. This may be due to the fact that Ms. Elliott had recently been hired and discovered too late that the numbers were low and that there were limited cash reserves. The academic year enrollment varied from 60% in some classrooms, with waiting lists in others.

Ms. Elliott prepared a full report on the financial concerns of the organization and presented it to the Board of Directors in a 2-hour meeting. (See her slides at the end of the case.) To date, Rising Hope is over $45,000 in debt. This includes a bank loan, secured to pay off bills, and the recently accrued invoices. The previous director had alluded to a cash reserve of around $50,000. When the annual audit was completed at the close of the year, no cash reserves were found. It seems that the cash reserve had been used to pay current bills, and the Board of Directors had not been informed of this appropriation. In addition, United Way funding has been decreasing due to the shrinking resources of the United Way Agency. (Currently, United Way funding accounts for 30 to 39% of the operating budget.) In summary, Rising Hope remains in a negative cash flow.

The Board of Directors usually addressed the financial reports only once or twice a year, since day-to-day operations were the responsibility of the director. Many members of the board found it hard to believe that Rising Hope could be in debt. It seemed to most of them that it was only one person's interpretation of doom and gloom. They would meet again in four weeks.

The next day, Mary left for the Daycare 2000 conference in Orlando, Florida. After spending time with other daycare directors, attending seminars on the latest developments and ideas in the industry, and lounging on the beach for an afternoon, Mary had time to consider her position. She figured that without a major plan—the center would be closed by the fall term. She would have to do crisis management and teach the board how to run a business rather than social service agency.

Mary discovered that Rising Hope was like many other centers, with payroll making up 60 to 62% of the operating budget. She also learned that the average cost per child per week of care was estimated to reach $125.00 within the next 18 months. Mary also attended sessions on enrollment policies and cash flow strategies. She found that most centers were requiring a full week's fees for a deposit. Many daycare centers were also breaking out meal fees and charging those separately so state food aid could be calculated.

Mary also found new ways to create additional revenue beyond childcare. In one instance, a center in the Midwest was combining childcare with well eldercare. It seems that the children and elderly helped one another, and it provided a positive experience for both groups. In addition there was a high profit and good revenue base on these types of programs. Another center had turned its kitchen operations into a family dining experience Monday through Thursdays evenings. For $5.00 a person, the family could eat together and not have to clean up the dishes. Several centers talked about how extending their hours of operation served to pull in a new base of parents who worked further away from the centers and had longer commute times. Other centers were also adding Saturday hours for shopping and group kid's play.

Returning from the conference, Mary concluded that the eldercare program should be the first plan to be developed. The resources and people were already in place, and licensing is not nearly as complicated as childcare licensing. Often times eldercare can also utilize insurance policies in order to ensure timely payments of fees. Mary plans to pitch this idea to the board along with a general fund-raising campaign. A primary issue still remains the ability to forecast revenue with a sliding fee scale, although eldercare could provide a more structured fee scale. Her main concern is that the board will automatically reject non-traditional options.

Rising Hope
Daycare
Making it . . .

The Stakeholders

- **The Children**
- The Board
- The Staff
- The Families
- The Community
- The Interim Investors

We Believe in . . .

Quality Affordable
Childcare

Current Enrollment
by Room

- Room #1 (3yr olds) 12/12
- Room #2 (4yr olds) 21/21
- Room #3 (prekinder)21/21
- Room #4 (Kinder) 16/23
- School Age 10/15

TOTAL
  70/77 Full time
  10.5/15 School Age

Cost Per Child
Per Week Average

National Average $92.00 a week

Mass. Average $101.00 a week

State Reimbursement Rate $74.00

Rising Hope Daycare $106.64

 Total operating budget
77 students

Budget for 1995
(January-December)

Total Proposed Operating Budget
$426,986.58

Labor $281,461.58 (65.9% of total budget)
    1994 Labor $234,452.48
    Increase of $ 47,009.10

Benefits $60,775.30 (14.2% of total budget)

Insurance	$24,975.30
FICA	$21,000.00
Unemployment	$11,000.00
Worker's Comp	$ 3,800.00

(For every $1.00 of salary we pay $21.59 in benefits)

All Other Expenses $84,750.00

    (To include food, liability insurance, utilities,
    classroom supplies, and all others)

United Way Contributions

1994--Community Care $105,703.00
1994--Designated Donor $ 4,978.65
             $110,681.65
    $27.64 per child/per week

1995--Community Care $ 96,899.00
1995--Designated Donor $ 3,547.70
             $100,446.70
    $25.09 per child/per week

Difference--Reduction

    Community Care $8,804.00
    Designated Donor $1,430.00
            Total $10,234.95
        $2.56 per child/per week

Room #1
3 yr olds/School yr
12 students Income Flow

$45.00 * 2 students = $ 90.00
$60.00 * 3 students = $180.00
$70.00 * 1 student = $ 70.00
$74.00 * 4 students = $296.00
$80.00 * 1 student = $ 80.00
$100.00 * 1Staff = $000000
    Total Revenue $716.00wk
Expenses
    $526.78 Staff
    $115.89 Tx/INS/Ben
    $ 45.00 JIPTA
    $ 20.00 Sch Supplies
    $120.00 Meals $2*5day(12)
    $897.24 Expenses wk
    Loss per week $111.67

Room #2

4 yr old/School yr

21/21 Students Income Flow

$33.75	1(2 child discount)	$ 33.75
$45.00	12	$540.00
$50.00	1	$ 50.00
$60.00	2	$120.00
$70.00	1	$ 70.00
$75.00	2	$150.00
$100.00	staff 1 child	000000
$74.00 4(State)		$296.00
Total Revenue		**$1259.75**

Expenses

$641.76   Staff(2)
$141.18   Tx/Ins/Ben
$ 45.00   JIPTA
$ 10.00   Foster Grandparent
$20.00   School Supplies
$210.00 Meals $2 *5 days (21)
$1067.94 Expenses

$191.81 Revenue per week

Room #3

Prekinder/School Yr
21/21 Students Income Flow

$33.75	2(2 child discount)	$ 67.50
$45.00	8	$360.00
$55.00	1	$ 55.00
$60.00	1	$ 60.00
$100.00	3	$300.00
	no staff	000000
$74.00 7(State)		$518.00
Total Revenue	**$1360.50**	

Expenses

$652.55   Staff(2)
$143.56   Tx/Ins/Ben
$ 45.00   JIPTA
$ 10.00   Foster Grandparent
$20.00   School Supplies
$210.00 Meals $2 *5 days (21)
$1081.11 Expenses

Revenue per week $279.39

38 weeks * 279.39 =10616.82

Room #4
Kindergarten/Sch yr

16/23 students Income Flow

$33.75 1(2 child discount)	$ 33.75
$45.00 3	$135.00
$50.00 1	$ 50.00
$60.00 3	$180.00
$70.00 1	$ 70.00
$75.00 2	$150.00
$74.00 5(State)	$370.00
Total Revenue	**$988.75**

Expenses

$586.40   Staff
$129.00   Tx/Ins/Ben
$ 45.00   JIPTA
$ 10.00   Foster Grandparent
$ 20.00   School Supplies
$230.00 Meals $2 *5 days (23)
$1020.40 Expenses

$31.65 Revenue per week

School Age Actual

School yr

10.5/15 students

Income Flow for Week 2/13

$25.00 1(2 child disct)	$25.00
$30.00 3(part-time disct)	$90.00
$50.00 1(full rate)	$50.00
$37.00 3(DHS/State)	$111.00
$50.00 3 (staff $50.00 (2))	000000
Total Revenue	**$276.00**

Expenses

$265.02 Salary Staff
$ 58.30 TX/INS/Ben
$ 45.00 JIPTA
$20.00   School Supplies
$ 75.00 Meal $1*5days(15)
$463.32

Loss of $187.32 a week

School Age $$$$
MAX. Possible
School Year

15 students *$50.00=$750.00 wk

Expenses

$265.02 Salary Staff
$ 58.30 TX/INS/Ben
$ 45.00 JIPTA
$20.00 School Supplies
$ 75.00 Meal $1*5days(15)

$463.32

Revenue per week $286.68

38 weeks*$286.68= $10,893.84

School Age
Max. Possible
Summer

15 students * $65.00=$975.00wk

Expenses

$ 265.02 Staff
$ 58.30 Tx/INS/Ben
$ 45.00 JIPTA
$ 20.00 Sch Supplies
$150.00 Meals $2*5day(15)

Total $538.32

$65.00 1 Staff child discount
$32.50 1 2-child discount

Revenue per week $339.18

11 weeks * $339.18 =$3730.98

Overhead Cost
Per Child/Per Week

Direct Costs

(all classrooms by classroom)

$235,560.52

Difference from Operating Budget

$191,426.06

(divide by 77 children/52 weeks)

Cost per child/per week for overhead

$47.81

Cost per child
per week/by room

Room direct cost +overhead

Room 1

$74.77 +$47.81=**$122.58**

Room 2

$50.85 +$47.81=**$98.66**

Room 3

$51.48 +$47.81=**$99.29**

Room 4

$44.37+$47.81=**$92.18**

(23 children)

$63.78+$47.81=**$111.59**

(16 children)

Competition's Rates

Fox

$70.00-110.00 per week

Increase Fall $80.00-130.00

Boston Day Nursery

$70.00-130.00 per week

Increase planned

[$103.20 cost per child/per week]

- *Quest to keep low end of the scale close to the State reimbursement.*
- *Re-qualify clients on sliding scale twice a year.*

Estimated Income

Forecasted Income

United Way Comm	$96,899.00
United Way Desg. D.	$ 3,547.70
State/CFC Desg	600.00

Projected

DHS/State/Pathways	$80,919.00
Child Foodcare Prgm	$35,900.00
Parent Fee Income current fees	
	$170,000.00
Grace Center Rent	$ 9,600.00
Other Gov Income	$ 2,000.00
Scholarship Income	$ 2,500.00
Total	$401,965.70

Funds Needed
to make it . . .

Projected Operating Budget $426,986.58

Estimated Income $401,965.70

NEED/Shortfall **($ 25,020.88)**

## 12

THE MUSKRAT ISLAND YACHT CLUB

Background

The Muskrat Island Yacht Club opened in 1964 as a private club. It was founded by two doctors and three lawyers, who wanted docking space for their yachts and a place to gather for socializing. The founders and their friends felt there was a need for a different type of recreational club on the lake, as the majority of other clubs in the area catered to hunters and fishermen.

The original concept was funded by the investment of $10,000 each from the initial 50 members. These founding members of the club were promised substantial input in the planning and development of the club, as well as rotating seats on the Board of Directors. In addition, they were allowed discounts on membership fees. Many chose to invest for the potential tax benefit.

The board purchased a large lot on a small island in Lake Michigan for the location for the Yacht Club. The property, which represented 60% of the total island acreage, was purchased for

$300,000. Although Muskrat Island was referred to as an island, in reality it is an isthmus, connected to the main land by a two lane road. On the waterfront side of the property, a dock with slips for 30 boats and mooring sites for an additional 40 boats were planned.

The only existing building on the lot was a large cottage that had operated as a diner for the past 5 years. The diner, named the Dockside, catered mostly to the fishermen who docked their boats nearby. The proprietor of the diner, Debbie Butler, and her family lived on the second floor of the cottage.

The purchase of the property was negatively received by many in the local community. The quiet, tight-knit community had been untouched by trendy development. There were no condominiums, no gourmet restaurants, and no tourist shops. To many, the purchase of the property represented a threat to the traditional way of life they valued.

By far, the worst publicity stemmed from the closing of the Dockside Diner and the requirement that Debbie Butler and her family vacate the premises immediately. The Butler family had rented the diner and their living quarters from the previous owner on a month-to-month basis and were aware that the property had been placed on the market. However, in spite of the forewarning, the diner operator protested through a series of letters to the editor and local posters, warning that "... big city tycoons were taking over our little town ..." In the interest of making the residents more comfortable, the Yacht Club developers launched a counter-campaign using a series of newspaper articles, posters, and flyers.

The development plan for Muskrat Island called for upgrading the present dock and moorings to accommodate members' boats. In addition, the building on the property would be renovated as a restaurant/clubhouse. This, the club founders proposed, would provide summer jobs for local young people, as well as increased spending at town shops. They stated repeatedly that they had no intention of interfering with the character of the community.

After 18 months of renovations, the club opened for its first season, (late April through early November), boasting a total of 125 members. Over the years, the property changed to meet the needs and desires of the members. In 1973, a pool and tennis courts were added. These developments were quickly followed by a pool-side lounge and an exercise spa.

1978 was a major turning point for the Muskrat Yacht Club. Dr. Carl Bessara, a founding member of club, died suddenly, and left the Yacht Club Corporation $8 million dollars. This bequest was targeted to be used for development of the Yacht Club as a first class recreation and lodging facility, which would be accessible to both members and non-club members. Over the years, the club had begun to lose members due to the limited amenities offered. The Muskrat Yacht Club did not provide members with services such as fine dining, lodging, catering, or meeting space. Dr. Bessera's bequest allowed the development of the Yacht Club as a multifaceted property.

By April of 1982, the development of the property was complete. Today, the Muskrat Island Yacht Club operation is comprised of a Marina with 193 boat slips, a full time Marina Management staff, 150 Guest Suites, used primarily by Yacht Club members and their business associates, and assorted small conferences. A pool, hot tub spa, and a wading pool are also included. Food and beverage services include: the Cabana Pool Side snack bar, open 11 a.m. to 9 p.m. with an average of 210 checks per day, two restaurants—the *Fore & Aft Room* (108 seats, 1.2

turns, bar with 19 seats), open for dinner only and specializing in fine continental cuisine; and the *Catamaran Cafe* (85 seats, 2.4 turns), serving breakfast, lunch, and dinner.

The property employs three full time staff members, who live on site year round; Marina Manager—David Gill; Executive Chef—Frank Mullany; and Maintenance Engineer—Pete Smith. When the property was renovated, both in the 1970s and 1980s, the housing accommodations above the main kitchen, comprised of 6 large rooms and two full baths, were maintained to provide housing for key staff members. The remainder of the Yacht Club staff is employed seasonally. Yearly salary for these full-year employees is calculated at $238,000.

Beginning in late March, a number of locals are employed in preparation for the season, which begins in mid- to late April, depending on the weather. The majority of the locals continue to work at the Yacht Club through the property closing in November.

During the peak of the season, the core staff is supplemented by college students and additional seasonal employees. College students primarily fill front of the house positions, whereas housekeeping, maintenance, grounds, laundry, transportation, dish-washing, and food production positions are filled by the remaining employees.

The Muskrat has been fortunate to have the majority of the in- seasonal employees return for several years in a row. In fact, there have been very few occasions when help wanted ads have been placed. Usually, a new employee is recommended by a current employee. This has been the case especially with the non-local seasonal employees who have tended to be international, and speak little or no English.

Housing for seasonal employees is provided on site. A separate wing, facing the guest suite wing of the property, has been reserved for employee housing. Some of the rooms are equipped with kitchenettes, while the majority are typical hotel rooms. Over the years, there have been relatively few issues related to employee housing in close proximity to guest rooms, with two exceptions. The first was related to a pest infestation that stemmed from an employee keeping food in his room without refrigeration, while the second centered around overly rowdy college-age employees who streaked through the guest quarters at 2:00 a.m. In both cases, the employees involved were immediately discharged.

The Muskrat Yacht Club currently boasts a membership of 526. Annual membership fees are $2,500 for facility use, and a 30% discount on the rack rate during both peak and non-peak seasons. Members wishing to dock their boats at the Club facilities may do so without a fee, whereas non-members are charged an annual fee of $1,500 per year. Non-members rent 45% of the boat slips each year. Founding members of the club and members serving on the 23-member board are granted a 50% discount on fees and services provided by the Yacht Club.

The occupancy for the hotel property has been maintained at 73% during the non-prime season (May, September, October, and November). During the peak summer months (June, July, and August), the rate increases to 84%. The rack rate is $95.00/double occupancy in the peak season, and $85.00/double occupancy during non-peak. At all times, 90% of guest rooms are blocked for member reservations. The Muskrat consistently sells out every weekend (Friday to Saturday), Memorial Day through Labor Day.

The average guest check in the Fore & Aft Restaurant is $19.75, in the Catamaran Cafe is $8.00 and at the Pool Side lounge is $12.00. Sixty percent of sales at the lounge are attributed to frozen cocktails. Catering is provided for many of the yachts for intimate dinners, cocktail parties, and receptions. There is also a substantial amount of business from small- to medium-sized companies that use the facility for training seminars, incentive reward weekends, and planning retreats. Catering activity yields a seasonal revenue of $204,000.

The local community has tolerated the development. As the bulk of business is concentrated in the summer months, the Muskrat Island Yacht Club provides valuable summer employment for the young people of the area. In addition, many of the young people return home from college each summer to work at the Yacht Club, something that did not occur prior to the development of the property as a resort destination. The majority of local residents agree that the management and the Board of Directors of the Muskrat Yacht Club have remained sensitive to the desires of residents.

However, in recent years, a group called Citizens Against Losing Muskrat —CALM—has been working to place limitations on the further development of the Yacht Club. The core of the group is comprised of local residents who have been financially hurt by the development and past employees dissatisfied with the management practices. As a result of the Yacht Club development, property values have increased as wealthy non-residents have purchased land for development as luxury summer homes. This has occurred on both the island and on the main shore This has led to large numbers of young families being driven out of the area, as real estate prices have risen dramatically.

In addition, the local labor pool has diminished somewhat, and Muskrat Yacht Club has employed more and more non-residents each year, the majority of whom are non-college students. These workers are paid less per hour than residents in return for on-sight housing. CALM has been very vocal about their objections to this practice. They have been concerned by the "exploitation of these workers" and have compared their employment terms to those of migrant farm workers. However, Letters to the Editor of the local paper have pointed out the substantial income generated by the Muskrat's presence not only from in-town spending by guests and the Multiplier Effect, but also from the 7% property tax paid on the $8,000,000 property and the $11,000 per year paid in Liquor Licensing fees.

A major turning point in this dispute occurred on a busy Saturday night in July. The restaurants were full to capacity, several catering functions were going on, and the lodge was operating at 100% occupancy. At approximately 8:45 p.m., the property was inspected by several Immigration and Naturalization Service (INS) officers. They were responding to an anonymous tip that many of the workers at the property were not work authorized.

The arrival of the officers back of the house prompted a mass exodus from the kitchen area. Workers abandoned food in the midst of production and fled in fear of arrest. The INS agents then proceeded to the employee housing wing where several people were arrested in full view of the guest rooms.

The raid left several large ripples in its wake. Guests had been disturbed by the ruckus raised as the undocumented workers were apprehended. Most of the workers who were arrested had family members or close friends who were legally working for the Muskrat Yacht Club. As a result, productivity in the days following the raid was affected considerably. Guest complaints increased 20% in the two-week period following the event. The majority of the complaints stemmed from prolonged waits for services and the lack of cleanliness of rooms and public space.

Publicity also created problems for the Muskrat. Echoes of past negative press emerged, as headlines in the paper screamed charges of unfair labor practices, indentured servitude, and prejudice. The majority of those impacted by the sting were Irish and Eastern-block undocumented workers.

The fine to be levied against the Muskrat Yacht Club stem from the cited violations, which included employment of undocumented workers and failure to maintain proper employment records, had yet to be communicated. The Board was understandably disturbed, not only by the raid and the impending fine, but also because of the trust they had placed in the property General Manager, Chibu Ngawbarrua.

Mr. Ngawbarrua's leadership over the years had been excellent. The Muskrat Yacht Club had consistently earned profits above projected levels, guest satisfaction ratings were exceptionally high, and over 80% of the staff were multiple-year seasonal employees, lending great stability to the operation. Other expenses were also very well managed. Advertising had been maintained at 2% of sales, Direct operating expenses at 7%, Repair and Maintenance at 2%, and Utilities at 4.2%. Depreciation is budgeted at 1.2% per year.

Mr. Ngawbarrua had also instituted strict controls in managing costs. He had re-negotiated annual insurance rates to $60,000, down from a previous high of $77,000. Knowing that managers would be more motivated not to exceed targeted costs if they were held personally accountable for departmental performance, Mr. Ngawbarrua created a compensation structure for managers that rewarded quality performance and penalized managers whose departments did not achieve targets in revenue, costs, and profits. Target costs for the Food and Beverage department are 36%. The Rooms division seeks to maintain a cost per room of $12.50 and the Marina maintains its costs at 30%. Because of Mr. Ngawbarrua's fine performance, the Board had long treated him with both the utmost respect, and had given him carte blanche in decision making.

The recent problems with employment practices, the resulting negative publicity, and guest dissatisfaction created a high level of concern for many Board members. Members were split between two camps. One camp felt that since Mr. Ngawbarrua's track record had been excellent, that he should be left alone to handle this problem. If problems were not corrected, they argued, the result would be that Mr. Ngawbarrua would not realize his bonus. This, they argued, provided sufficient motivation for Mr. Ngawbarrua to get the organization and publicity back under control.

Meanwhile, others on the Board felt strongly that Mr. Ngawbarrua should be held accountable for the events at the Yacht Club, both personally and financially. These members felt betrayed by Mr. Ngawbarrua, because he had obviously broken the law by hiring these illegal workers. They felt Mr. Ngawbarrua should be placed on written notice, his negotiated bonus seized, and his contact terminated at the end of its term if profits and guest satisfaction did not increase.

After several meetings, the Board came to agreement and met with Mr. Ngawbarrua. He was informed that the bonus structure for the current season had been terminated. Furthermore he was given an ultimatum, to pull the organization back into compliance with INS regulations, increase profitability and guest satisfaction, and resolve public relations issues with the community. If these objectives were achieved within two seasons, his contract would be considered for renewal. In addition, if the fine levied against the Muskrat were to be assessed at more than $10,000, the

Board would once again re-examine terms of Mr. Ngawbarrua's employment status.

These terms left Mr. Ngawbarrua in a difficult position. In part, his successful management of the Yacht Club was tied to holding payroll expense below 23% of sales. During the current season, payroll expenses were running 20.3%. However, Mr. Ngawbarrua was not intimately involved in the hiring of staff. Rather, he allowed individual department heads to manage their own employee affairs. He reasoned that there was not a pressing need to oversee these functions because (a) things were running so well, and (b) most employees were seasonal, so a formal Human Resource Department would be a wasteful expenditure. Further complicating issues, was the fact that Mr. Ngawbarrua was quite sure that the tip to INS had come from a current employee, a fact that he did not share with the Board.

13

THE GEORGIA HOTEL

Background

The Georgia Hotel has been a landmark property in the greater Atlanta area for more than 50 years. The Georgia has 534 rooms, easy access to Interstate 20, and serves a combination of business clientele and leisure travelers. In anticipation of the Olympic games, the property has recently been renovated. Herman Eissen, General Manager, has worked for this organization for the past 15 years and is nearing retirement. Herman has spent his career focusing on the lodging side of operations, and has seen this property through two renovations. Marlene Rutledge has been the Assistant General Manager for 22 months and has earned excellent reviews. Marlene, unlike Herman, is not from the area, coming originally from Peoria, Illinois. Marlene had prior experience with brand name properties such as Holiday Inn and Ramada Inns, and her area of expertise is in food and beverage operations.

The Georgia has held a steady 62.8% annual occupancy rate for the past three years and is sold out of all rooms at least 90 days a year. The Butler Room is a 154-seat restaurant/bar with a large dance floor and is located on the second floor of the hotel. The Grand Magnolia Ballroom, with seating for up to 800 people, breaks into 4 separate function rooms, each seating between 120 and 250 people. On Sunday mornings, the Ballroom is used to serve a "southern champagne brunch" for $14.95. This price is a dollar more than other competing brunches in the area to reinforce its quality. The price value is still high given the average food cost per brunch is 37%. They often serve upwards of 900 people on Sundays. The Tara Coffee Verandah seats 60 people and does the majority of its sales as carry-out business. The menu consists of baked goods and coffees. The Tara Coffee Verandah closes at 2 p.m. and reopens at 9 p.m. The Georgia provides room service from 5 a.m. until midnight. Additionally, the hotel has six board rooms available, each seating 18 people.

Herman has made great efforts over the years to draw the local community into the restaurants in the hotel. He has worked hard to build up the business on weekends in the Butler Room by bringing in live entertainment. His primary objective was to choose some entertainment which would allow him to maximize his alcohol sales, and to increase his guest check by at least $15 a couple. Herman has been able to take advantage of local talent and a couple "big name bands." His objective this month is to turn over the entertainment decision making for the Butler Room over to Marlene. He needs to decide if he will recommend her as General Manager when he retires.

Herman admits that he's had some less than successful moments in the Butler Room, like the time he used singing waiters. The guests loved the entertainment, but didn't drink as much or order as many appetizers as when he had a musical group in the bar. Marlene said she had a similar experience in the lounge at the Holiday Inn when she had used singing bartenders. Her only problem was that the bartenders were more interested in their tips than in up-selling. Thanks to Herman's experience, the hotel is in the practice of including a contract rider, regarding conduct in the hotel, in all contracts for musicians. Herman is willing to share all his entertainment records with Marlene and wants to review her plans for January and February entertainment in the next two weeks.

The area newspapers and media have always given the Butler Room favorable food reviews. The chef is known for his creativity, and it has always been perceived as elegant dining. Over the past two years Herman has concentrated on booking the groups. He has learned that customer feedback is not as valuable to him as checking the bottom line. Herman has typically evaluated entertainment on a individual group basis and has not developed a full plan since this effort is independent of the business plan developed with the owners.

The planning for the Georgia Hotel has always been done with the owner, the general manager and the director of marketing. The marketing plans have always emphasized rooms and special weekend packages. In the last three years, the marketing campaign has also included promotion of the Sunday and holiday brunches. Everyone felt it was a better value to attract local people in the area, rather than the spend big dollars on television advertisements. The local radio stations of WJZF, WGST, WKLS, WNNZ, and WPCH are very competitive, with 30-second spots running between $450 and $700 per 30-second spot. The area newspapers give deep discounts for repeat customers, with full page ads costing between $11,000 and $20,000, depending on the paper and the day of the week. The market research suggests that most of the room business is determined by people who are within a 12-mile radius of the property, even if the guest is from out of the region.

Local businesses within 12 miles are being targeted for promotions. Last year the Georgia Hotel had 14.7 million dollars in room revenue and 3.65 million dollars in food and beverage operations.

In a conversation with Herman, Marlene planned to ask many questions during the first time through the planning process. Here is the memo listing Marlene's questions about entertainment plans for the Butler Room:

To: Herman Eissen

From: Marlene Rutledge

Date: November 3, 1995

Subject: Entertainment Planning for the Butler Room

I have been investigating the entertainment issue for the Butler Room. Here are some of the questions I've encountered. I'd like to discuss these tomorrow at our 1 p.m. meeting.

▲ Based upon the "entertainment worksheets," what groups showed the best profit?

▲ How would you classify the types of entertainment? ... 1 hour shows with breaks; dance evenings; comedians; Singing Broadway Dinner shows; or Murder Mystery Dinners.

▲ Should we look into Sports Events?

▲ Have we done theme menus to go with the type of entertainment?

▲ How far ahead do we sign contracts and how do we screen the entertainment?

▲ Are our customers the same, regardless of the type of entertainment?

▲ How does the owner feel about our efforts to develop a weekend entertainment market?

- ▲ Have we looked at entertainment which could also increase our table turns?
- ▲ Do we have a special reservation systems—have we ever needed one?

Many thanks for your help.

Summary of Entertainment

The Georgia Hotel -- June-September 1995

Group Name	Weekend	Nights Played	Total Revenues	Net Profit (loss)	% of Profit	Notes
Bravo Broadway	2-Jun	Fri./Sat	$3,939	$481	12.21%	older local crowd
Bravo Broadway	9-Jun	Fri./Sat	$4,718	$757	16.04%	good alcohol sales
Bravo Broadway	23-Jun	Fri./Sat	$4,654	$328	7.05%	repeat crowd
Bravo Broadway	30-Jun	Fri./Sat	$4,924	$370	7.51%	good dessert sales
Bravo Broadway	7-Jul	Fri./Sat	$4,167	$598	14.35%	repeat crowd
Bravo Broadway	14-Jul	Fri./Sat	$4,405	$876	19.89%	good dessert sales
Angela Bacari	21-Jul	Fri./Sat	$3,587	($705)	-19.65%	cost of special equip $560
Angela Bacari	30-Jul	Fri./Sat	$3,045	($993)	-32.61%	room night comp—full house
Angela Bacari	4-Aug	Fri./Sat	$4,050	($449)	-11.09%	room nights comp—full house
Crossroads	11-Aug	Fri./Sat	$4,846	$80	1.65%	nice weather—cool
Crossroads	18-Aug	Fri./Sat	$3,763	$436	11.59%	lots of dessert drinks
Ecstasy	25-Aug	Fri./Sat	$4,004	($464)	-11.59%	large group of 40
Corky May & Coalition	1-Sep	Fri./Sat	$5,185	$165	3.18%	large glass breakage
Windsong	8-Sep	Fri./Sat	$4,729	$1,566	33.11%	Warm-up group for T. Keith
Windsong	15-Sep	Fri./Sat	$4,888	$1,865	38.15%	Most sales apps. & bevs.
Windsong	22-Sep	Fri./Sat	$4,418	$1,302	29.47%	Most sales apps. & bevs.
Crossroads	29-Sep	Fri./Sat	$6,101	$207	3.39%	Make up for illness
TOTAL From Entertainment -- June-Sept			$75,423	$6,420	8.51%	

Mulit-Dimensional Hospitality Operations

Entertainment Worksheet

The Georgia Hotel

Date_____					This Year	Last Year
Day_____						
INCOME	Food Sales					
	Beverage Sales					
	Total Sales				_____	_____
	Advance Reservations					
	Final Cover Count					
EXPENSES	Cost of Food	Percentage				
	Cost of Beverages	Percentage				
	Advertising					
	Radio Station	# of Spots	Length	Dates Run	Cost	
				Total Radio	_____	
	Newspapers	# of Inserts	Spread	Dates Run	Cost	
				Total Newspapers	_____	
	Labor					
		# of Hours	Avg. Rate	Total Wages		
	Prep cooks					
	Dishwashers					
	Waitress(s)					
	Hostess					
	Bartender					
	Management					
			Benefits 20%	_____	Total Wages _____	
	Posters					
	Direct Mailers	Postage/Printing				
	Promotional Giveaways					
	Decorations					
	Menu Printing					
TOTAL EXPENSES						
Operating Profit (Loss)						

14

AMERICAN FILM STUDIO & BAR

Denver, Colorado

How It All Started

The American Film Studio & Bar started its operation in the Early Spring of 1994 in downtown Denver, Colorado. Paul George and John Joseph were college roommates who loved movies and food. Both men earned business degrees from the University of Houston. They kept in touch over the years and after 10 years of successful employment decided they wanted to own a business together. Both men were married and wanted to move their families away from the big city chaos, yet they still wanted metropolitan convenience. Denver, Colorado, was the ideal fit for their business and family dreams. Between the two men they had $120,000 cash and good credit ratings.

Paul and John decided to focus on the restaurant entertainment business. After looking over the distressed properties downtown, they decided to rent the third floor of a building built in 1940s. It already had a comedy club on the second floor. They decided to hire someone with hospitality education and at least 5 years of restaurant experience to manage the operation and focus on the food service operations. After a 3-week interviewing process, they found Kate Beginn, who had graduated from FIU and had worked at TGIFRIDAYS for seven years. Kate fit right in with Paul and John's way of thinking and profit orientation. The three of them decided to take the bar concept with food, and use movies as the form of entertainment. Eight months later, the American Film Studio & Bar was started, after about $80,000 worth of renovation and $20,000 of advertising. The film distributors were pleased to supply, at a fair price, second-run films for this new venture.

Restaurant & Theater

The American Film Studio & Bar shows second-run movies and serves alcohol and food during the movie. The property has two theaters, with two showings each night per theater. The first seating/showing is at 6:15 to 6:45 p.m. Monday through Thursday with the second showing at 9:30 to 9:45 p.m. No one under the age of 21 is admitted because alcohol is served on the property. The weekend has 3 showings on Fridays, Saturdays and Sundays. On the weekends there are 6:15 p.m., 9:30 p.m., and 12:15 a.m. showings, with Saturday and Sunday having an additional matinee in the afternoon at 3:15 p.m. Each theater seats up to 300 people. Every person purchases a movie ticket for $3.00. There is also a minimum purchase requirement of one item of any kind per-person/per-show. As the tickets are sold, total audience size is forecasted to the restaurant staff and relayed via walkie/talkie. Reservations can be taken for groups of five people or more by calling ahead. There is a waiting area with a large brass bar where drinks can be purchased while waiting to be seated. The theater is opened 10 minutes before the showing, and the entire waiting room is seated in a 5 to 7 minute period, using the waitstaff as ushers. There are two levels to each theater, with smoking on the upper level and non-smoking on the lower level. The layout in the smoking section consists of round tables of two tops and four tops. All traffic flow down to the lower level is through the smoking section. On a cold windy day, ventilation is effected and the lower level can become smoky. Two/thirds of the way through the show an intermission is planned—just at an exciting moment, during which "last calls" on drinks is given. There are 5 to 8 waitstaff to serve each theater, depending on the number of guests. There is a maximum of 2 separate checks allowed at each table in order to minimize talking during the movie. The wait staff has been trained to be very unintrusive. They kneel down at the tables and whisper to take orders during the movie. They also keep free refills taken care of so that no guest ever has less than a half-empty glass. Service is such that the waitstaff takes orders at each table right before the movie begins. Line time on all menu items is less than 12 minutes so that prompt service can be assured. One central kitchen is used to service both theaters.

There is an extensive frozen drink menu (prices between $4.00 and $6.50), plus an extensive appetizer list including items between $4.95 and $6.95. Also available are a number of deli baskets with fries or chips (running $4.95 each). A sampling of the sandwich selection includes hot pastrami, seafood salad, marinated vegetable sandwiches, and grilled chicken. The wine and beer selection offers bottled beers and domestic wines with a price range of $2.95 to $3.95 for beers and $3.50 to $4.50 for wines.

While old buildings have great character, they have some drawbacks. There are only two washrooms with four stalls in each. There is always a line during the intermission and after the show. During the restoration, a "yellow brick road" was painted from the elevator to the theater booth to cover the badly scuffed floor. The zoning by the city could have been a problem, but, luckily, this distressed property was not protected by the historical society. Generally, tax breaks are available on the old buildings, as was the case here. There is a parking garage adjacent to the building. A parking validation program was worked out where parking is discounted to $1 with a stamped ticket from the American Film Studio & Bar. The parking garage is glad to have the regular business, and the increased awareness of the garage has helped its overall business. There are also two revamped shopping areas downtown within two blocks of the American Film Studio & Bar. Sports events are also common in the nearby sports arena. The convention center is only four blocks away.

Internal Promotions

The following internal promotions are available:

Business Card Fish Bowl—The American Film Studio & Bar invites people to submit their business cards for a weekly drawing, where 20 cards per day are drawn for people to choose a movie and a Monday/ Tuesday or Wednesday/Thursday. The person whose card is drawn is given a choice of several dates and several movies. Each business card fish bowl winner may bring 10 guests for free admission, with a minimum purchase of one item per person.

Birthday Bashes—For the month of your birthday, you get 20 free passes to be used Monday through Thursday with reservations. A free mini birthday cake, serving six, is provided. Additional cakes may be purchased for $5 each. For advanced orders, the

American Film Studio & Bar will put the person's name on the cake. After you sign up, you are sent a reminder card for the month of your birthday.

Frequent User Club—This $30.00 package includes one movie pass, good for four people, any day of the week, and a free T-shirt. A special keychain is provided and serves as the electronic pass to the movies. American Film Studio & Bar wants to encourage people to come here for dining.

Old Movie Club—Classic old movies are shown in one theater every Tuesday. For $25, people can purchase a one-year pass, good for up to four people. This also includes a free mug featuring a character from an old movie. They also receive the key chain which provides the electronic pass to the movies. This promotion is also designed to encourage people to come here for dinner.

Movie Store—posters, mugs, drink glasses of all shapes and sizes for all kinds of drinks, T shirts, keychains, brain-teaser toys, water globes, magnets, hats, beach towels, movie themed salt and pepper shakers, and old movie books are available in the lobby. An item from the Movie Store is featured on the tables for purchase each week. The delicate items are held under a glass case on each table. The waitstaff are able to sell all items from the Movie Store. The Movie Store runs off a separate register and operating budget.

Advertising

Advertising is done in a variety of ways. The primary advertising is done in the phone book under restaurants and movies, and in the movie advertisements sections of the local newspaper. Direct mailings are sent to people who sign up for the mailing list on a monthly basis. Another successful service is the fax-back form, where American Film Studio & Bar sends you the featured movies of the week via fax. There is also a phone system with an answering machine giving a listing of movie times, and a separate line for making reservations.

Four to five nights out of the week, DJs from local radio stations provide an introduction to the movie, tell jokes, and give away promos from the station. Occasionally, the comedy club will send up a comedian for 10 to 15 minutes before a movie begins.

Meal Specials

The head bartender works to develop new drink specials to fit the theme of the movie being shown. The specialties of the house are usually ice cream drinks or mixes. The beverage costs are maintained in a 19 to 21% range at all times. Beverages sales are a key part of the concept. The kitchen manager always works with the head bartender to put together a food and drink combination promotion for the night. Each waiter tastes the newly created drink specials, and as a perk of the job, receives the evening special for a meal. There is very little turn-over in the waitstaff, with the average waiter clearing between $80.00 to $120.00 a night.

Two Years of Success

Two years of success with the property in Colorado have Paul and John thinking about franchising this concept in major metropolitan areas which are experiencing growth. Each year the business has grown, with over $325,000 a year profit. Their lawyer has drafted a solid franchisee agreement. John attributes much of their success to Kate's ability to optimize the purchasing and training. Kate spends close to 40 hours a month working with the vendors and distributors to get the best quality and the best price. Often times she has been told that if she just had more volume, the discount and services would increase.

The most significant costs are under tight operational control. The food costs are 29.5 to 30%. Labor costs are steady at 23%. Administration and general costs are $200,000 a year. The promotional budget operates as close to break-even as possible, allowing up to a $40,000 in expenses per year. Monthly rent is $6,400.00. Direct operating expenses are 7%. The average week at the American Film Studio & Bar yields approximately $100,600 in revenue. A separate business unit has been set up for the *Movie Store*, making it a sub-unit of the promotional budget.

Overall, Paul and John found no direct competitors in the market after their first two years. It seems that as far as food operations go, the local downtown business is growing for lunch and fine dining, but there are very few bars open serving the same clients. Many of the guests coming in like the combination of food, drink, and a movie for the evening. The HipHop, across the street, serves burgers, appetizers, and drinks, and has been open for three years, serving lunch and dinner. Both the American Film Studio & Bar and HipHop have similar clientele, but both seem to be doing well. There are two food courts in the nearby malls, which primarily serve quick service items such as pizza and fast food chinese. The nearest first-run cinema theater is over 8 miles away. The refurbished mall re-opened its cinema and is showing a full schedule of 6 movies, but the selections are very different from this operation. The American Film Studio & Bar is easily accessible off of the interstate and the main streets for downtown traffic. Business is really good, and profits have been more than originally anticipated. Paul and John are active in the business, with Kate handling the food operations.

Paul and John have decided to hold back the franchise option until they see if the purchasing plan can be developed and added to the agreement. They have asked Kate to draft a "wish list" they can put out to bid, to see if they can increase the profitability of the operations.

Kate has submitted for their discussion the following items to consider:

▲   Training programs for all management, bar staff and waitstaff. MTV-type video training programs for the staff, support manuals, and semi-annual updates to all campaigns.

▲   Seek out additional vendor's purchasing power by strategic alliances such as an ice cream (such as Ben & Jerry's) or bakery line (such as Pillsbury).

▲   Promotional marketing of beverages, campaigns the customers will recognize, and all promotional materials needed, with possible tie-ins to national marketing campaigns.

▲   Availability of product and service of the accounts to minimize inventory necessary on hand.

Paul and John agreed to focus on these items in the bid process for the beverage purchases in the American Film Studio & Bar. They will seek bids for alcohol purchases of five times the current volume within the next twelve months. Their goal is to open five franchises West of the Rocky Mountains by the end of this year, and no later than twelve months from now. The question remains on how and whether to proceed with this design.

Promotional Audit

Annual/1996 Forecasted	Quarter 1	Quarter 2	Quarter 3	Quarter 4	Total
Sales					
Birthday Bashes(cakes)	$1,800.00	$1,800.00	$1,800.00	$1,800.00	$7,200.00
Frequent User Club	$13,650.00	$13,650.00	$13,650.00	$13,650.00	$54,600.00
Old Movie Club	$8,325.00	$8,325.00	$8,325.00	$8,325.00	$33,300.00
Movie Store	$27,450.00	$30,120.00	$26,850.00	$39,840.00	$124,260.00
				TOTAL	$219,360.00
Cost of Sales					
Business Card Fish Bowl					
tickets	$7,200.00	$7,200.00	$7,200.00	$7,200.00	$28,800.00
postage/printing	$423.00	$423.00	$423.00	$423.00	$1,692.00
Birthday Bashes					
tickets	$3,600.00	$3,600.00	$3,600.00	$3,600.00	$14,400.00
cake	$75.00	$75.00	$75.00	$75.00	$300.00
postage/printing	$2,557.27	$2,557.27	$2,557.27	$2,557.27	$10,229.08
Frequent User Club					
tickets	$1,260.00	$1,260.00	$1,260.00	$1,260.00	$5,040.00
T-shirts	$2,217.60	$2,217.60	$2,217.60	$2,217.60	$8,870.40
keychain	$147.00	$147.00	$147.00	$147.00	$588.00
postage/printing	$1,175.00	$1,175.00	$1,175.00	$1,175.00	$4,700.00
Old Movie Club					
tickets	$2,040.00	$2,040.00	$2,040.00	$2,040.00	$8,160.00
T-shirts	$3,570.00	$3,570.00	$3,570.00	$3,570.00	$14,280.00
keychain	$238.00	$238.00	$238.00	$238.00	$952.00
postage/printing	$752.00	$752.00	$752.00	$752.00	$3,008.00
Movie Store					
postage/printing	$3,760.00	$3,760.00	$3,760.00	$3,760.00	$15,040.00
T-shirts	$3,250.00	$3,250.00	$3,250.00	$3,250.00	$13,000.00
keychain	$148.50	$148.50	$148.50	$148.50	$594.00
posters	$465.00	$465.00	$465.00	$765.00	$2,160.00
glassware	$225.00	$225.00	$225.00	$225.00	$900.00
brain-teaser toys	$600.00	$600.00	$600.00	$600.00	$2,400.00
water globes	$1,200.00	$1,200.00	$1,200.00	$1,200.00	$4,800.00

Annual/1996 Forecasted	Quarter 1	Quarter 2	Quarter 3	Quarter 4	Total
Movie Store Cont.					
hats	$850.00	$850.00	$850.00	$850.00	$3,400.00
beach towels	$350.00	$350.00	$350.00	$350.00	$1,400.00
salt & pepper shakers	$125.00	$125.00	$125.00	$125.00	$500.00
old movie books	$950.00	$950.00	$950.00	$950.00	$3,800.00
				TOTAL	**$47,994.00**
Advertising				**Total Promo**	**$149,013.48**
Phone Book	$122.00	$122.00	$122.00	$122.00	$488.00
Answering Machine	$55.00	$55.00	$55.00	$55.00	$220.00
Newspaper	$15,000.00	$15,000.00	$15,000.00	$15,000.00	$60,000.00
Direct Mailers— nonprogram	$5,640.00	$5,640.00	$5,640.00	$5,640.00	$22,560.00
Faxback Supplies/Phone	$125.00	$125.00	$125.00	$125.00	$500.00
				Total Adv	**$83,768.00**
Promo rev-costs	($13,421.48)				

Daily Revenues

American Film Studio & Bar, Monday—Thursday

Monday—Thursday Week 37—August 1996	Theater 2 Show 1	Theater2 Show 1	Theater 2 Show 1	Theater 2 Show 2	Daily Total
Monday					
Number of Guests	135	210	180	280	805
Number of Advance Registrations	50	40	25	50	165
Number in Birthday Group	0	5	0	15	20
Number in Fish Bowl	50	40	50	30	170
Movie Sales	**$255.00**	**$495.00**	**$390.00**	**$705.00**	**$1,845.00**
Food Sales					
Appetizers	$657.23	$1,008.36	$1,197.00	$1,167.36	$4,029.95
Sandwiches	$99.00	$215.00	$178.20	$150.63	$642.83
Desserts	$59.25	$23.65	$86.90	$47.89	$217.69
Total Food Sales	**$815.48**	**$1,247.01**	**$1,462.10**	**$1,365.88**	**$4,890.47**
Beverage Sales					
Frozen	$148.84	$231.53	$198.45	$308.70	$887.51
Specials	$168.75	$262.50	$225.00	$350.00	$1,006.25
Beer	$126.23	$196.35	$168.30	$261.80	$752.68
Wine	$78.98	$122.85	$105.30	$163.80	$470.93
Mixes	$109.01	$169.58	$145.35	$226.10	$650.04
Non-alcohol drinks	$105.14	$163.55	$140.18	$218.06	626.934
Total Beverage Sales	**$736.94**	**$1,146.35**	**$982.58**	**$1,528.46**	**$4,394.33**
TOTAL DAILY REVENUE	**$11,129.80**				
Tuesday					
Number of Guests	186	225	188	300	899
Number of Advance Registrations	44	85	25	90	244
Number in Birthday Group	8	7	11	22	48
Number in Fish Bowl	40	50	50	50	190
Movie Sales	**$414.00**	**$504.00**	**$381.00**	**$684.00**	**$1,983.00**
Food Sales					
Appetizers	$569.16	$688.50	$575.28	$918.00	$2,750.94
Sandwiches	$184.14	$222.75	$186.12	$297.00	$890.01

American Film Studio & Bar, Monday—Thursday

Monday—Thursday Week 37—August 1996	Theater 2 Show 1	Theater2 Show 1	Theater 2 Show 1	Theater 2 Show 2	Daily Total
Food Sales, cont.					
Desserts	$80.82	$97.76	$81.69	$130.35	$390.62
Total Food Sales	**$834.12**	**$1,009.01**	**$843.09**	**$1,345.35**	**$4,031.57**
Beverage Sales					
Frozen	$205.07	$248.06	$207.27	$330.75	$991.15
Specials	$232.50	$281.25	$235.00	$375.00	$1,123.75
Beer	$173.91	$210.38	$175.78	$280.50	$840.57
Wine	$108.81	$131.63	$109.98	$175.50	$525.92
Mixes	$150.20	$181.69	$151.81	$242.25	$725.94
Non-Alcohol drinks	$144.86	$175.23	$146.41	$233.64	700.1412
Total Beverage Sales	**$1,015.34**	**$1,228.23**	**$1,026.25**	**$1,637.64**	**$4,907.46**
TOTAL DAILY REVENUE	**$10,922.03**				
Wednesday					
Number of Guests	222	250	244	299	1015
Number of Advance Registration	66	64	48	88	266
Number in Birthday Group	8	11	7	21	47
Number in Fish Bowl	50	30	50	40	170
Movie Sales	**$492.00**	**$627.00**	**$561.00**	**$714.00**	**$2,394.00**
Food Sales					
Appetizers	$657.23	$1,008.36	$1,197.00	$1,167.36	$4,029.95
Sandwiches	$99.00	$215.00	$178.20	$150.63	$642.83
Desserts	$59.25	$23.65	$86.90	$47.89	$217.69
Total Food Sales	**$815.48**	**$1,247.01**	**$1,462.10**	**$1,365.88**	**$4,890.47**
Beverage Sales					
Frozen	$244.76	$275.63	$269.01	$329.65	$1,119.04
Specials	$277.50	$312.50	$305.00	$373.75	$1,268.75
Beer	$207.57	$233.75	$228.14	$279.57	$949.03
Wine	$129.87	$146.25	$142.74	$174.92	$593.78
Mixes	$179.27	$201.88	$197.03	$241.44	$819.61
Non-alcohol drinks	$172.89	$194.70	$190.03	$232.86	790.482

American Film Studio & Bar, Monday—Thursday

Monday—Thursday Week 37—August 1996	Theater 2 Show 1	Theater2 Show 1	Theater 2 Show 1	Theater 2 Show 2	Daily Total
Thursday					
Number of Guests	247	245	199	288	979
Number of Advance Registration	55	150	75	66	346
Number in Birthday Group	12	5	12	20	49
Number in Fish Bowl	60	50		50	50
Movie Sales	**$525.00**	**$570.00**	**$411.00**	**$654.00**	**$2,160.00**
Food Sales					
Appetizers	$755.82	$749.70	$608.94	$881.28	$2,995.74
Sandwiches	$244.53	$242.55	$197.01	$285.12	$969.21
Desserts	$107.32	$106.45	$86.47	$125.14	$425.38
Total Food Sales	**$1,107.67**	**$1,098.70**	**$892.42**	**$1,291.54**	**$4,390.33**
Beverage Sales					
Frozen	$272.32	$270.11	$219.40	$317.52	$1,079.35
Specials	$308.75	$306.25	$248.75	$360.00	$1,223.75
Beer	$230.95	$229.08	$186.07	$269.28	$915.37
Wine	$144.50	$143.33	$116.42	$168.48	$572.72
Mixes	$199.45	$197.84	$160.69	$232.56	$790.54
Non-alcohol drinks	$192.36	$190.81	$154.98	$224.29	762.4452
Total Beverage Sales	**$1,348.32**	**$1,337.41**	**$1,086.30**	**$1,572.13**	**$5,344.17**
TOTAL DAILY REVENUE	**$11,894.49**				

American Film Studio & Bar, Friday—Sunday

Friday—Sunday Week 37—Aug. '96	Theater 1 Show 1	Theater 2 Show 1	Theater 1 Show 2	Theater 2 Show 2	Theater 1 Show 3	Theater 2 Show 3	Daily Total
Friday							
Number of Guests	222	250	244	299	288	220	1523
Number of Advance Registrations	166	58	150	189	140	88	791
Number in Birthday Groups	8	11	7	21	5	0	52
Number on Fish Bowl	0	0	0	0	0	0	0
Movie Sales	**$642.00**	**$717.00**	**$711.00**	**$834.00**	**$849.00**	**$660.00**	**$4,413.00**

American Film Studio & Bar, Friday—Sunday

Friday—Sunday Week 37—Aug. '96	Theater 1 Show 1	Theater 2 Show 1	Theater 1 Show 2	Theater 2 Show 2	Theater 1 Show 3	Theater 2 Show 3	Daily Total
Number on Fish Bowl	0	0	0	0	0	0	0
Movie Sales	**$642.00**	**$717.00**	**$711.00**	**$834.00**	**$849.00**	**$660.00**	**$4,413.00**
Food Sales							
Appetizers	$679.32	$765.00	$746.64	$914.94	$881.28	$269.28	$4,256.46
Sandwiches	$219.78	$247.50	$241.56	$296.01	$285.12	$87.12	$1,377.09
Desserts	$96.46	$108.63	$106.02	$129.92	$125.14	$38.24	$604.39
Total Food Sales	**$995.56**	**$1,121.13**	**$1,094.22**	**$1,340.87**	**$1,291.54**	**$394.64**	**$6,237.94**
Beverage Sales							
Frozen	$244.76	$275.63	$269.01	$329.65	$317.52	$242.55	$1,679.11
Specials	$277.50	$312.50	$305.00	$373.75	$360.00	$275.00	$1,903.75
Beer	$207.57	$233.75	$228.14	$279.57	$269.28	$205.70	$1,424.01
Wine	$129.87	$146.25	$142.74	$174.92	$168.48	$128.70	$890.96
Mixes	$179.27	$201.88	$197.03	$241.44	$232.56	$177.65	$1,229.82
Non-Alcohol drinks	$172.89	$194.70	$190.03	$232.86	$224.29	$171.34	$1,186.11
Total Beverage Sales	**$1,211.85**	**$1,364.70**	**$1,331.95**	**$1,632.18**	**$1,572.13**	**$1,200.94**	**$8,313.75**
TOTAL DAILY REVENUE	**$18,964.69**						
Saturday							
Number of Guests	247	245	199	288	277	254	1510
Number of Advance Reservations	55	171	88	69	57	188	628
Number in Birthday Groups	12	5	12	20	8	9	66
Number in Fish Bowl	0	0	0	0	0	0	0
Movie Sales	**$705.00**	**$720.00**	**$561.00**	**$804.00**	**$807.00**	**$735.00**	**$4,332.00**
Food Sales							
Appetizers	$755.82	$749.70	$608.94	$881.28	$847.62	$777.24	$4,620.60
Sandwiches	$244.53	$242.55	$197.01	$285.12	$274.23	$251.46	$1,494.90
Desserts	$107.32	$106.45	$86.47	$125.14	$120.36	$110.36	$656.10

Multi-Dimensional Hospitality Operations

American Film Studio & Bar, Friday—Sunday

Friday—Sunday Week 37—Aug. '96	Theater 1 Show 1	Theater 2 Show 1	Theater 1 Show 2	Theater 2 Show 2	Theater 1 Show 3	Theater 2 Show 3	Daily Total
Bev. Sales, cont.							
Beer	$230.95	$229.08	$186.07	$269.28	$259.00	$237.49	$1,411.85
Wine	$144.50	$143.33	$116.42	$168.48	$162.05	$148.59	$883.35
Mixes	$199.45	$197.84	$160.69	$232.56	$223.68	$205.11	$1,219.33
Non-alcohol drinks	$192.36	$190.81	$154.98	$224.29	$215.73	$197.82	$1,175.99
Total Beverage Sales	**$1,348.32**	**$1,337.41**	**$1,086.30**	**$1,572.13**	**$1,512.09**	**$1,386.54**	**$8,242.79**
TOTAL DAILY REVENUE	**$19,346.38**						
Sunday							
Number of Guests	287	278	190	189	149	129	1222
Number of Advance Registrations	120	58	124	54	36	56	448
Number in Birthday Groups	2	6	3	5	0	0	16
Number in Fish Bowl	0	0	0	0	0	0	0
Movie Sales	**$855.00**	**$816.00**	**$561.00**	**$552.00**	**$447.00**	**$387.00**	**$3,618.00**
Food Sales							
Appetizers	$878.22	$850.68	$581.40	$578.34	$455.94	$171.36	$3,515.94
Sandwiches	$284.13	$275.22	$188.10	$187.11	$147.51	$55.44	$1,137.51
Desserts	$124.70	$120.79	$82.56	$82.12	$64.74	$24.33	$499.24
Total Food Sales	**$1,287.05**	**$1,246.69**	**$852.06**	**$847.57**	**$668.19**	**$251.13**	**$5,152.69**
Beverage Sales							
Frozen	$316.42	$306.50	$209.48	$208.37	$164.27	$142.22	$1,347.26
Specials	$358.75	$347.50	$237.50	$236.25	$186.25	$161.25	$1,527.50
Beer	$268.35	$259.93	$177.65	$176.72	$139.32	$120.62	$1,142.57
Wine	$167.90	$162.63	$111.15	$110.57	$87.17	$75.47	$714.87
Mixes	$231.75	$224.49	$153.43	$152.62	$120.32	$104.17	$986.77
Non-Alcohol drinks	$223.52	$216.51	$147.97	$147.19	$116.04	$100.47	$951.69
Total Beverage Sales	**$1,566.68**	**$1,517.55**	**$1,037.17**	**$1,031.71**	**$813.36**	**$704.19**	**$6,670.65**
TOTAL DAILY REVENUE	**$15,441.34**						

15

THE BRICKCOURT HOTEL

Meet Mr. Taylor

Carson Taylor was appointed General Manager of The BrickCourt Hotel in Motard, California 6 months ago. The property, which first opened in 1918, has been very successful over the years, but in the wake of economic downturns, social changes and population shifts, the past 10 years have seen a steady decrease in both revenues and profitability. Mr. Taylor was hired by the property owners in an attempt to reverse the downward spiral. His ability to reposition historic properties in distressed locations was well known, and successful property recoveries in Providence, RI., Fairfax, VA., and Kansas City, MO., demonstrated Mr. Taylor's skills. His educational background is an interesting one. Mr. Taylor originally enrolled in college as a Pre-Med student. However, mid-way through his senior year in college, he changed his course of study to that of Business and ultimately earned a MBA degree from the Wharton School at the University of Pennsylvania.

After graduation, Mr. Taylor was employed by Cooper-Lybrand for several years. During this time he worked on a variety of company projects including several that involved the hospitality industry. It was through this introduction to the industry, that Mr. Taylor discovered his love of hospitality. He left Coopers-Lybrand to pursue a career in the industry. Throughout the 1980s, Mr. Taylor held a variety of positions at hotels throughout the country. Each position he obtained carried with it greater and greater responsibility.

His skills as a manager and his keen financial and strategic planning ability became highly sought after. Mr. Taylor became known as the "Turnaround King" because of his success in rescuing ailing historic properties from bankruptcy, and, ultimately, the wrecking ball. It was this reputation that led the owners of The BrickCourt to recruit Mr. Taylor as General Manager, and to charge him with the development of a strategic plan for the historic hotel within 6 months of his appointment.

The BrickCourt Hotel: Stay with Us, Experience the History

The BrickCourt Hotel was built in the heyday of Motard, California. Motard is a secondary city located in Southern California. During the late 1800s through the mid-1900s, the city was a bustling center of business and travel. Many people passed through Motard on their way to Los Angeles, Santa Barbara, and San Diego. The city was an important stop for the railroad and later for buses traveling to the major cities on the coast.

Through the economic boom years, the population and business centers grew aggressively. Located on the outskirts of downtown, The BrickCourt was one of the centers of both social and business life in the community. The 200-room hotel provided not only exceptional room accommodations for the time, but also boasted a world class restaurant, complete with a French chef, as well as banquet rooms and separate gathering salons for women and men. The BrickCourt was THE place to stay in Motard.

The location of the hotel was ideal for both business and pleasure travelers. The close location to the business center made The BrickCourt the ideal home-base for businessmen, while the lovely park across the road from the hotel provided opportunity for recreation. Just outside the hotel's main doors was a 45-acre park, complete with flower gardens, a promenade, a man-made lake, and a small zoo. This provided hours of entertainment for hotel guests, as well as an exceptional view for guests staying at the hotel.

Over the years, however, the nature of the city changed substantially. As fewer people traveled by train or bus, the number of visitors coming into the city decreased dramatically. Business growth in Motard plummeted as businesses and newer hotels chose to locate closer to airports. This trend, in turn, triggered a movement of the population away from the city and into the new suburban areas, which were springing up around the airports.

As a result, downtown Motard became economically depressed. The once dynamic downtown became a semi-ghost town and property values plummeted. The BrickCourt saw not only its occupancy, but also its reputation, plummet. Crime began to increase in the area, the park became the residence of many homeless persons, and the hotel was rimmed by several rundown buildings.

The BrickCourt had remained in private ownership over the years, and paid off its mortgage in full in 1958. From time to time, offers were made by other hotel companies to purchase the property, but each time they were rejected. In more recent years, the offers have been few and far between, in part because of the hotel's location.

In 1983, the hotel owners seriously considered closing the property and selling the building. However, the local historical society was working very hard to rejuvenate the downtown with the cooperation of several public and government agencies. Through these efforts, The BrickCourt was granted funds to rehabilitated the aging property. In 1981, the property underwent a $1,000,000 renovation that concentrated on electrical, heating, and structural repairs, rather than cosmetic repairs. A fund-raising effort to "Preserve The BrickCourt" was led by a private citizens group in 1984, and over the years the money raised allowed for repairs to the wallpaper and painting, gold leaf, and marble staircases.

Despite the repairs, the occupancy did not improve. The park across the street was still noted for crime, and funds being raised for park repair project were short of the $6,000,000 target. However, the neighborhood was changing. The decrease in property values made the purchase of large parcels of land more affordable. Fountain Hospital, a teaching and research hospital, had been looking for a location where it could consolidate its present organization into one large campus, rather than being between nine area buildings.

As Fountain developed its newly purchased property, within a block of The BrickCourt Hotel, the occupancy rate at the hotel began to gradually increase. Throughout the mid-1980s and into the early 1990s this trend increased. Initially, planners and consultants stayed at the property, and then as the new facilities opened, the property began to serve the families of patients. The arrangement was mutually beneficial to both The BrickCourt and Fountain Hospital.

Another Year Like This, and The BrickCourt Will Be History

Over the last year and a half, a number of events have seriously endangered the continued operation of The BrickCourt Hotel. These challenges have come in the form of decrease occupancy from patient families, due to the opening of a Family Hostel on the hospital campus, repeated attempts by the Fountain Hospital to buy out the hotel property, and attempts by the local historical society to place the hotel on the National List of Historic Places.

One year before Carson Taylor came to The BrickCourt Hotel, Fountain Hospital converted one of the buildings on its property into a low-cost hostel to provide families with an additional alternative to the hotel. Many patients and their families had complained over the years that the cost of staying at The BrickCourt Hotel, at $85.00 per night, was prohibitive. Attempts to negotiate a lower rate for families of patients were rejected by the hotel management initially, but eventually settled at a reduced rate of $70.00 per night. The hotel's occupancy rate averaged 52% per year, with 72% of the total business coming from patient familes.

The Fountain Family Hostel was formally a men's athletic club. It is a turn of the century building, providing 25 guest rooms, shared baths, and no cooking or meal facilities. Families staying at the Hostel are encouraged to dine at the hospital cafeteria. Since its opening, the Fountain Family Hostel has operated at 97% occupancy.

Given the success of the Hostel concept, the Fountain Hospital set its eyes on the BrickCourt property. With the hotel's 200 rooms, food and beverage facilities, and private baths, it would be an ideal location for a new and improved Family Hostel. In addition, relocation of the Hostel would allow conversion of the present Hostel facility into a dormitory for medical residents. However, recent budget cuts resulting from decreased reimbursement by the government and medical insurance companies, coupled with shorter hospital stays, had caused the hospital board to scrutinize additional property investment very closely. As a result, the offer to purchase the BrickCourt for $1.5 million dollars was one that the owners of The BrickCourt could easily pass up. The low bid was carefully calculated by the hospital board. It was their expectation that while the offer was rejected today, the continued poor performance of the property would result in the owners of the BrickCourt reconsidering and ultimately accepting the offer.

The local Historical Society, meanwhile, had been lobbying for the designation of the hotel as an historical landmark. Initially, the proposal seemed to be ideal. If appointed as an historic landmark, The BrickCourt would be entitled to certain grant moneys as well as a fair degree of protection. In addition, there was an opportunity to highlight the special status in terms of marketing strategies. However, as with most things, these positive outcomes did not come without drawbacks. Once accepted as an historic landmark, the freedom to renovate the interior and exterior of the building would be virtually eliminated. Changes to both the cosmetic and the physical structure of the BrickCourt would be subjected to review by the local board of the Preservation Society. The owners of the hotel were wary of giving up this freedom.

Carson Taylor Proposes Two Plans

The days leading to Mr. Taylor's 6 month anniversary at The BrickCourt Hotel passed quickly. He spent hundreds of hours becoming acquainted with not only the facility, but also with the people who worked at the property, the local community, and business leaders from Motard and its surrounding cities. Carson Taylor firmly believed that one could not make valid recommendations for a property's future without fully immersing oneself in both the operations and the surrounding community.

Over the months, Mr. Taylor careful crafted two plans to bring forward to the owners of The BrickCourt Hotel. His analysis of the current business climate confirmed that status quo would lead The BrickCourt to closure within 5 years. It would take bold, aggressive, and committed action to turn the property around, and it was with this theme in mind that Carson Taylor went to the owners with his proposals.

Carson Taylor met the owners of the property and their lawyer in the lobby of The BrickCourt Hotel and escorted them to a private boardroom on the second floor. Once pleasantries were exchanged and everyone was comfortable, Mr. Taylor took his place at the head of the table and began his presentation. In his opening remarks, he commended the owners for their commitment to preserving the property and for their wisdom in hiring him. The remark generated laughter from the group.

He continued by introducing the parameters within which he had developed the two plans for the future of The BrickCourt. Number one was the concern that the property could not tolerate a repositioning plan that would take longer than 180 days to come to fruition. A tight cash flow prohibited a longer implementation plan.

Second, Mr. Taylor voiced his commitment to retain the character of the property. He intended to do this by preserving key facets of the hotel such as the lobby, the quaint sitting clusters with couches and chairs through out the lobby and on each floor, and the hotel's reputation for food and beverage excellence. "The BrickCourt Hotel has a magnificent past," he continued, "and it is up to us to ensure her future. It is with that goal in mind, that I bring the following proposals for your consideration."

Plan I

The BrickCourt - Your Home Away from Home

Mr. Taylor's first proposal outlined a position change from a commercial hotel property to a blended concept where a portion of the hotel property would be maintained as a commercial operation, and the balance of the property would be converted into long-term stay or resident-leased accommodations. This approach would have two major advantages, the first being that the nature of the physical plant would not need to be significantly altered. Second, the provision of extended-stay options would attract some of the patient families from the Family Hostel operated by Fountain Hospital. Taylor's research of patient family staying at the Fountain Family Hostel indicated that the vast majority would be willing to pay a somewhat higher rate for accommodations at The BrickCourt, which included private baths, continental breakfast, and food and beverage facilities. These services, combined with a 24 hour shuttle to the hospital, would form the basis of the amenities package for extended stay patrons.

Multi-Dimensional Hospitality Operations

Furthermore, Mr. Taylor presented the idea of leasing rooms on the top floor of the hotel on an annual basis, turning the top of the hotel into small apartments. Services to the apartment residents would include maid and laundry service. By renting these "apartments," which would need to be converted to accommodate kitchenettes, a steady base of income would be guaranteed. Mr. Taylor described four main types of clients renting these apartments. The first groups would be doctors from Fountain Hospital, who would use the apartment as a secondary residence. The second group would be older people, who no longer wanted to be bothered with the maintenance and upkeep of their houses. The third and more interesting group would be people who were nostalgic about the heyday of The BrickCourt. Yet another possible group would be the local companies that required accommodations for traveling executives several times a year.

The remainder of the hotel would remain a commercial hotel operation. Mr. Taylor proposed the following sales mix: 40 rooms (floor 6) residential apartments, 60 rooms (floors 4 and 5) extended stay, and a 100 rooms (floors 2, 3, 4) commercial hotel rooms.

Room Type	# of Type	Projected Occupancy		Room/Rental Rates
		Yr.1	Yr. 2	
Residential Apartments leases to be negotiated annually	40	50%	90%	$950 per month
Extended Stay	60	84%	89%	$350 per week
Standard Commercial	100	72%	74%	$90.00 per night double/ single occupancy.

This diversified approach, he argued, would allow The BrickCourt to maintain its historical identity as a commercial hotel, while creating two additional products. However, the renovation of the top floor into apartments is expected to cost $45,000. These costs are related to the installation of kitchenettes, separate phone lines, and other changes required by local building and housing codes. Discussions with City Hall had revealed no obstacles to the plan with regard to zoning. Local architects had been consulted, and preliminary renderings of the apartment floor were presented to the group. Several minutes of discussion followed.

Plan 2

The BrickCourt Executive Spa/Wellness Center: The Perfect Getaway

In opening his second proposal, Mr. Taylor asked the group to put aside their traditional views of what services a hotel property should provide. The secret in business, he continued, is to challenge the status quo and be inventive in your appeal to your prospective customers. "The mid 1990s through the beginning of the 21st century will be a time when America ages, when company executives have less and less time and more and more stress, and as a direct result of Rightsizing, each Senior Executive will be critical to corporate success. The trend will be to work-until-you drop, in order to get ahead. But consider the implications for the major corporation when the CEO keels over and dies of a heart attack at age 52 or dies of a cancer that wasn't detected until it had reached advanced stages. It is in these potential tragedies, that The BrickCourt may find its future!" stated Mr. Taylor emphatically. Responding to the enthusiasm of the group, he continued the presentation, outlining his vision in detail.

"The mission of The BrickCourt Executive Spa/ Wellness Center," he continued, "will be to provide corporate executives with the best of two worlds— rest, relaxation, hospitality, AND the best medical services available. After a 3-, 5-, or 7-day stay at the BrickCourt, the executives and their families will leave feeling refreshed and confident, knowing that any health issues that might impact the executives ability to continue to work will have been identified, and a course of treatment begun."

To accommodate this second plan, the first floor of the hotel would remain vastly unchanged. The food and beverage facilities, sitting areas, gift shops and pool area would physically remain the same; however slight changes in philosophy would be required. The food and beverage outlets would alter their offerings to ensure that nutritional guidelines would be met. In addition, one of the gift shops in the lobby would be closed and be reopened as a tourist-travel service agency. The purpose of the new operation would be to facilitate travel arrangements to and from the Spa/Wellness Center and to arrange local side trips for the families.

However, substantial changes to the second floor of the hotel property would be necessary. The total reconstruction of this floor would be required to transform it from hotel rooms into a state-of-the-art medical facility, providing examination rooms, testing equipment, medical offices, and conference rooms. The entire floor would be leased to a team of medical specialists who would occupy the floor for fixed rate of $50,000 per year plus and additional 3% of total revenue from the medical service provided on site.

Executives in need of an annual physical or testing would check into the hotel, with or without their families. Families of the executives would be scheduled for events and entertainment during the day and would be reunited with the executive for dinner each day. Guest staying at the hotel would pay a rate of $210 per double/single occupancy, under a European plan. This increase in rate would cover the cost of meals provided. Some family side trips would be without cost, whereas others would require additional payment.

For the executive, the stay would begin with an in-depth interview, including a complete medical history and conference with the executive's personal physician, in person or over the phone. Next, an examination regime would be planned and the "rules" for the stay would be explained. Executives would be required to adhere to several guidelines during their stay, including limiting their contact with the office to 1 hour per day. During this contact, their heart rate would be monitored. In addition, executives would eat only the foods provided by the hotel's restaurants and room service, with outside "treats" being prohibited.

During the remainder of their stay, the executives would interact with a team of medical specialists designed to evaluate all facets of his/her health. This team would include an Internist, a Cardiologist, an Oncologist, an Orthopedic/ Sports Medicine Specialist, an Obstetrician/ Gynecologist, an Urologist, and a Psychiatrist. This team would be supported by Registered Nurses and Licensed Practical Nurses, a Medical Nutritionist, a Massage Therapist, and Personal Exercise Trainers. The philosophy of the Executive Spa/Wellness Center would be to evaluate current health, assess future health, and generate recommendations for an exercise and diet regime after leaving The BrickCourt.

All the medical doctors practicing at the Executive Spa/Wellness Center would be associated with Fountain Hospital. This would be critical in order to allow testing on expensive medical equipment such as CAT Scans or MRI testing. In addition, sophisticated medical tests and the filling of prescriptions would be completed by the hospital. Should an exam reveal a serious condition needing immediate intervention, the hospital would provide surgical and Intensive Care facilities.

Mr. Taylor revealed that he had done extensive research on the concept and the need for such services. He cited the Mayo Center in Minnesota had long operated a similar concept within a hospital center. What executive, he asked the group, would prefer to stay in a hospital in Minnesota rather than come to sunny California and stay in a comfortable historical hotel? Furthermore, he had spent much time discussing the concept with friends from his college years, including medical professionals and senior executives. Both groups had a positive response to the concept.

Conversion of the second floor would cost an estimated $950,000 and would take approximately five months. Architects projected little difficulty with the physical changes to the second floor, but recommended that the third floor be closed during renovations. The hotel could remain open, on a limited basis, during construction. Occupancy during construction has been estimated at 45%, during the first year of new operation at 58%, and, by year 4, the estimated rate would be 78%.

A Medical Administrator, similar to a Hospital Administrator, would be hired to oversee and coordinate the wellness program. The annual salary for this individual would be an estimated $50,000. Furthermore, substantial investment would be required to introduce the facility to both the medical and business communities. Mr. Taylor recommended a combination of approaches that would include print ads in magazines like Fortune and Money, booth presence at regional and national medical conferences, and incentive discounts for clients who would book their stays with The BrickCourt prior to its Grand Re-Opening.

Charting the Future from Here

The boardroom was silent at the end of this second proposal. Carson Taylor broke silence by sitting down at the table, folding his hands and clearing his throat. "I have presented two plans that I believe will provide a future for The BrickCourt Hotel. The fact is, that without a new approach, the hotel will fade into the history books within a few years. Furthermore, immediate action is necessary if some of the changes are to be made, as the placement of the hotel on the registrar of historical places would greatly complicate, if not prohibit, some facets of the two proposals. Ladies and Gentlemen, I await your decision."

_____
_____
_____
_____
_____
_____
_____
_____
_____
_____
_____
_____
_____
_____
_____
_____
_____
_____
_____
_____
_____
_____
_____
_____
_____
_____

16

Prairie Convention Center

Bloomington, Illinois

The Prairie Convention Center is a new concept being considered by the greater Bloomington/Normal and McLean County Department of Economic Development. McLean County is in the middle of the state of Illinois, half way between Chicago and St. Louis, at the intersection of Interstate 74 and Interstate 55. The cities of Bloomington and Normal are at the heart of this county which has primarily been known for its black rich soil and agriculture, State Farm Insurance Corporate headquarters, Diamond Star auto plant, Kathryn Beich's Candy of Nestle Co., and for the two universities of Illinois State University (ISU) and Illinois Wesleyan. The economy has traditionally been based on corn and soybeans. Over the last fifteen years there has been tremendous growth in the area. The population of the Twin Cities has grown from 120,00 to over 150,000. There is a great deal of new construction including homes, restaurants, motels, and budget hotel properties. State Farm Insurance has grown and purchased more land in the immediate Bloomington area. The Farm Progress Show was hosted in 1994 in McLean County, bringing hundreds of thousands of people to the area. The economic growth in the area is not by accident. The mayors and city managers of Bloomington and Normal have worked to attracts events they can uniquely serve, such as the annual Corvette Car Show, Special Olympics, McLean County 4-H Fair, Shakespeare Festival, and the Prairie Airshow, to name a few. The local radio station—WJBC has won top awards for listenership and impact upon the community.

The leaders are interested in creating Bloomington/Normal as a tourist destination. They want to make the most of the university students that come in and out of the area. There is great opportunity, given that Bloomington/Normal is at the crossroads of two major interstates. The planning teams believe they have significant regional opportunities since there is air and train access to Bloomington/Normal. Ultimately the strategy is to draw people into the Bloomington/Normal area as guests and then attract them as residents and business owners.

The leadership in the McLean county area does not believe it needs a consultant to help figure out the convention center issue. Many of the planners for the Bloomington/Normal area believe that no one could know the intimate opportunities and issues of the area better than this comprehensive team. Furthermore, everyone currently on the team is a stakeholder with commitment in the community. The struggle will be to balance their current position in the market with the potential they have in the market over the next 10 years. Building the Prairie Convention Center will have some risk, but it also has some great potential. The Prairie Convention Center team is made up of the mayors of Normal, Bloomington, LeRoy, and Lexington; the city managers of Bloomington and Normal; the local lodging/restaurant association officers; representatives from the Presidents' Offices of Illinois State University and Wesleyan; as well as leadership from the top ten employers in the area and the Farm Bureau leadership.

Over the last fifteen years, retail and outlet shopping centers have become available on both sides of the twin cities. In the past, the only major shopping area had been Eastland Mall, located on the east side of Bloomington. This led to the further development of the beltline/business Rt. 55 as the "restaurant row." As of June of 1996, Bloomington/Normal was adding a restaurant every week to the area with an annual average close to 50 a year. Major restaurant franchise operations are attracted to this area. Recently, TGIFridays has decided to share its property and build a Raddison Hotel on the same site. McLean county has also become a significant regional financial center with several banks anchored in Bloomington/Normal.

Through the use of newspaper and radio, the community is quite aware and supportive of the planning team. Local farmers have been heard describing how "we are modeling our area after the Indianapolis area." Everyone wants to find that small town atmosphere with the opportunities of the big town economics. Most people in the area feel the 4 major employers (State Farm Insurance, Diamond Star, ISU, and the Bromen Hospital) will remain stable. The addition of agriculture and geography to the mix should help to make Bloomington/Normal the next crossroads. Right now, the area is looking to attract something similar to the Indianapolis 500 that would draw great media attention to the area. It is believed that with the trends for the next millennium moving toward connections to the earth, the setting of McLean County is perfect. Consideration has been given to roads, traffic flow, and other infrastructure efforts, such as community centers. The greater Bloomington/Normal and McLean County area demonstrates a phenomenal amount of cooperation and teamwork in this effort—almost as if city boundaries are merely a token, and everyone is part of a greater community effort. All the literature out of the Department of Eeconomic Development is talking about all the towns and cities in the area, not just Bloomington/Normal. The marketing concept for the area is "We'd love your company." In the literature, meeting facilities are indexed by the location, availability, and size of the facilities, and include additional contact information.

Meeting Facility Capacity

Meeting Facility	Capacity	Fees
Ash Park Recreation Center	89	$50 first two hours; $10 each additional hour
Best Western Eastland Suites Lodge	500 (depending on setup)	Vary
Best Western University Inn	35	With service
Bloomington Public Library	25, 150	Non-profit group, $20/hour max of $50; Others, $20/hour, max of $150
Bloomington Sale Barn	5,000	Vary
Comfort Inn	25	$50/day
Courtyard Marriott	25-30	$75/half day; $125/whole day
Crestwicke Country Club	10-125 meeting; 250 dinner	$50-$250/day
Davis Lodge	200 standing	$75/day
Days Inn East	50	$55
Ewing Manor	60-200	Vary
Fairfield Inn	6-75	$50-200/day
Gridley Village Hall	25	Negotiable
Hampton Inn	20 people	$45-75
Holiday Inn	28-650	Vary

Meeting Facility	Capacity	Fees
Illinois State University—Bone Student Center	12-3,400	Vary
Illinois State University—Redbird Arena	10,000	Vary
Jumer's Chateau	10-500	$75-$400
Ironwood Golf Course	130	$50 for non-profit group; $200 1st hour, $15/extra hour others
Knights of Columbus	15-200	$250/day
LaFayette Club	650/seated	Vary
Lexington Community Center	25-150	Main room—$75 for first five hours, $15/hr thereafter; small meeting room—$30/first five hours, $15/hr thereafter
McLean County Fair Grounds	10-800	Various
McLean County Farm Bureau Building	120-160	$140 for entire day; $120 for evening only
McLean County Historical Society	150	Fees vary by organization and events taking place
McLean County Law & Justice Center	40-50	No charge unless used after hours and on weekends
Miller Park Pavilion	250-325	$240/day for non-profit groups; $480/day for business use
National Guard Armory	400	Vary
Normal City Hall—council chambers	81	None
Normal City Hall—Conference Room	50	None
Normal City Hall Annex I	56	$50 first two hrs; $10/hour thereafter
Normal Township Hall	75	$15-$50
Paragon Ballroom	520/seated	Vary
Personal Development Institute	150	Vary
Prairie Vista	128	$100 M-Th; $200 F-Sun

Meeting Facility Capacity, cont.

Meeting Facility	Capacity	Fees
Ramada Inn FundDome	10-200	$70-$400
Scottish Rite Temple	20-800	Vary
Signature Inn	5-85	$80-$150
Washington Square East	10-300	Per case (how long, how many, week or weekend)
Wesleyan Memorial Center	10-450	Vary

The city fathers are currently strategizing on the development of a convention center to coincide with the relocation of the county fairgrounds. The new fairground's location has a lot of room for expansion, while offering better interstate access and more parking. Given the current meeting facilities and the goals for the community, the question remains as to what type of facilities will be needed, if any, to bring in conference/meetings/tradeshows or other large groups. The last thing the planning team wants is to get stuck with a "white elephant" in the middle of farm country.

The decision making team includes the city councils for Bloomington and Normal as well as the McLean County leaders in the Office of Economic Development. They have put together an extensive home page on the Internet. This web page is organized into the following sections: Communities and Government, Organizations, Business, Events, Educational Institutions, Weather, Geography, History, Census, and Demographic links. The links available provide information on everything from upcoming events and lodging accommodations to the grain markets.

Several city council men and women suggested that the planners look at the total number of hotel rooms available in the area to see if there are any franchise hotel groups which would be willing to build an anchor for a convention center.

Right now, Indianapolis is the model for the Bloomington/Normal area. Indianapolis is one of the fastest growing cities in the country, with dynamic economic growth and an unemployment rate of less than 1%. The good news it that Indianapolis is 3 hours away, and almost equal distance for the Chicago market, while actually being further away from the St. Louis area. On the other hand, the city of Peoria is less than an hour away. The McLean county community leadership has watched over the last 20 years as the city of Peoria has struggled because of it single manufacturing focus. The city fathers of Bloomington/Normal and McLean County want to be sure they don't build the economy on shaky ground. They feel that diversity in employers and expansion into tourism/hospitality are the only ways to keep the area growing beyond the next ten years. This growth needs to be planned and controlled appropriately in order to create a solid tax base and a well-designed infrastructure of roads and utilities. The goal of the planning team is to address the Prairie Convention Center issue before the end of 1996

Lodging

Hotel/Motel	Rooms	Price
Best Inn Motel	107	$36
Best Western Eastland Suites Lodge and Conference Center	64 studio suites; 24 2- bedroom suites	$78-$100
Best Western University Inn	102	$51 Sun.-Thurs.; $58 Fri.-Sat.
Coachman Inn Motel	50	$30
Comfort Inn	103	$49.95
Days Inn East	100	$51
Days Inn West	58	$46.95
Fairfield Inn	127	$49.95 Sun.-Thurs; $59.95 Fri.- Sat.
Hampton Inn	108	$65-$71 Sun.-Thurs.

Lodging, cont.

Hotel/Motel	Rooms	Price
Hojo Inn	32	$42
Holiday Inn Bloomington-Normal	160	$69-$78
Jumer's Chateau	180	$80
L & L Motel	20	$26
Motel 6	98	$26-32
Ramada Inn FunDome	210	$58-67
Ramada Inn West	89	$45-50
The Rodeway Inn/Parkway Inn	100	$40-45
Signature Inn	124	$61
Super 8 Motel—Bloomington	62	$41.88-44.88
Super 8 Motel—Normal	52	$40

Bed and Breakfasts

The Burr House	2 guest rooms	Call for rates
Rose Manor	3 guest rooms	Call for rates

A great deal of lodging data and meeting facility information has already been collected. The new fair grounds are on the west side of the twin cities. The design of the buildings and the layout of parking and traffic flow are being evaluated to service more than just several thousand 4-H kids with livestock and other projects once or twice a year. Since growth is happening, it only makes sense that the greater Bloomington/Normal and McLean county area needs a plan. This would allow for bond issues, corporate sponsorship or some combination of efforts to create the financial structure to support the Prairie Convention Center.

Multi-Dimensional Hospitality Operations

Name: _____

Analysis & Investigation Sheet

Environmental Analysis —Perspective: _____
Internal Environment

#	Strengths	Weaknesses	#
	OPERATIONAL PRACTICES	OPERATIONAL PRACTICES	
	HUMAN RESOURCES	HUMAN RESOURCES	
	STRATEGIC PLANNING	STRATEGIC PLANNING	
	MARKETING	MARKETING	
	FINANCIAL	FINANCIAL	
	PHYSICAL PLANT	PHYSICAL PLANT	
	MISCELLANEOUS	MISCELLANEOUS	

©1997, Prentice-Hall, Inc.

Environmental Analysis —cont.

External Environment

#	Opportunities	Threats	#
	GUESTS	GUESTS	
	SOCIAL TRENDS	SOCIAL TRENDS	
	NATURE	NATURE	
	ECONOMY	ECONOMY	
	TECHNOLOGY	TECHNOLOGY	
	POLITICAL	POLITICAL	
	COMPETITION	COMPETITION	
	MISCELLANEOUS	MISCELLANEOUS	

Name: _____

Symptoms of the Problem

	Rank

Statement of the Central Problem

If properly identified, all symptoms will go away when the problem is solved.

_____

_____

_____

_____

_____

_____

_____

_____

_____

_____

Name: _____

Additional Information Desired

Extra information you wish you had in order to fully determine the problem.

▲ _____

▲ _____

▲ _____

▲ _____

▲ _____

▲ _____

▲ _____

▲ _____

Options

Description	Consequence
1. Status Quo	
2.	
3.	
4.	
5.	
6.	

Name: _____

Recommendation—Action Plan

Give a chronological action plan using as much authority as is necessary to solve the problem.

1.	Who?	What?
	When?	How?
2.	Who?	What?
	When?	How?
3.	Who?	What?
	When?	How?
4.	Who?	What?
	When?	How?
5.	Who?	What?
	When?	How?
6.	Who?	What?
	When?	How?

©1997, Prentice-Hall, Inc.

Summary of Recommendation

_____

_____

_____

_____

_____

_____

_____

_____

_____

Financial Issues

_____

_____

_____

_____

_____

_____

Name: _____

Summary of Financial Data

Financial Facts	Word Formulas
Time Interval	
Revenue	
Total Sales	
Cost of Sales	
Controllable Expenses	
Occupation Cost	
Profit Before Taxes	
Income Tax	
Net Income (loss)	